AF541754

Microcredit and Rural Poverty

MICROCREDIT AND RURAL POVERTY

By

Dr. M. Lakshmi Narasaiah
M.A., Ph.D.

Professor of Economics,
Co-ordinator, Department of M.B.A. and Commerce,
Special Officer,
Sri Krishnadevaraya University Post-graduate Centre,
Kurnool–518 002
Andhra Pradesh (India)

DISCOVERY PUBLISHING HOUSE
NEW DELHI

First Published-2006

Reprinted-2011

ISBN 81-8356-069-5

Published by

DISCOVERY PUBLISHING HOUSE

4831/24, Ansari Road, Prahlad Street,
Darya Ganj, New Delhi-110002 (India)
Phone: 23279245 • Fax: 91-11-23253475
E-mail:dphtemp@indiatimes.com

Printed at:
Mehra Offset Press
Delhi

Preface

Poverty can be overcome, and that the poor can increase their income and production within an appropriate framework. Part of that framework is made up of a flow of resources and local-level institutional development, and there is considerable scope for improvement in both. However, the impact of investment and organisation is strictly determined by the nature of the policy environment. While project and programmes can bring some relief to the rural poor, substantial change needs a strong policy commitment. While the poor can overcome poverty, they will not be able to until this becomes a major focus of national policy and action. In the main, this sort of commitment has not been made in the past—at the expense of both the poor and overall development in many areas.

The current state of India is highly contradictory. On the one hand, there is proclamation of a new order; on the other, increasing value is given to sectional and short-term national and group interests. With an overt concern with the India's poor goes an equal weight given to concern with economic mechanisms and relations that pay little attention to poverty and foster more inequality. The dangers of this situation are real. The lack of concrete attention being given to change will mean greater economic polarisation. Greater polarisation among the better-off, and between the better-off and the poor—means instability and a lack of consensus, a lack of legitimacy.

Poverty is far-reaching, and ought to be curtailed. In a period in which resources everywhere appear restricted, this seems not to be an attractive proposition at the practical level.

Welfare is everywhere giving way to production as an imperative, just as public expenditure is giving way to private accumulation. Poverty alleviation does not appear to be an idea whose time has come. The objections are great, but they are also misplaced. Poverty alleviation is not necessarily a drain upon accumulation, and it is not primarily a public activity. Poverty alleviation is primarily the activity of the poor themselves, and their progress necessarily involves productive expansion. If this potential for private expansion has not been realised, it is not because of the nature of the poor, it is because of the way in which national economic affairs have been organised. Economic policy has been oriented towards the better off—not infrequently at the expense of the poor. Given the historic association between wealth and power, the definition of development in terms of the large and the wealthy is hardly surprising.

There is the possibility of associated growth involving both large-scale and small-scale production, the better of and the poor. The realisation of this possibility might result from a new social compact. This social compact is not a commitment to social safety nets and welfare, both of which seem to presuppose that the poor are somehow necessarily out of the growth field. It is a commitment to abolishing artificial and onerous terms of exchange that discriminate against the poor, to investing resources where there are real opportunities for gain, irrespective of whether the economic agents concerned are rich or poor, and to creating the space for the poor to organise to pursue their social and economic interests.

There is a need for a new growth model consistent with new social realities. While the 1980s was a period of clearing away many of the obstacles to development, it was not a period in which there emerged a clear vision of what represented the positive basis for growth, beyond, that is, a general prescription of market-driven operations. The model must pass from admonition to positive prescription to fuel growth by integrating the poor in their rightful place in the production function. It must redefine the position of public expenditure in the development process, and seek to establish market structures which are both equitable and open to the participation of the economically weaker elements of the population. Most of all it must revalue the position and contribution of the poor and small-scale producers in the growth process, particularly in the agricultural sector, but not exclusively agriculture.

This means that the issue is not so much one of less government, but of government, both national and local, finding a new rationale for action, including, *inter alia*, creating conditions that will effectively unleash the productive potential of the rural poor.

Financial flows to the poorest Indians are not likely to undergo a very major expansion, especially through private channels. Development will rely very much on the mobilisation of their own resources, and many of these resources are in the hands of the poor, are, indeed, not only the human capital embodied in the poor but also their assets which, while small, individually are cumulatively important in India. The growth model for the 1990s will have to embrace that fact, and build upon it. The paradox of most development models is that they have emphasized the value of what Indians do not have, while devaluing what they have: capital intensity has been promoted in situations of scarcity of capital, at the expense of abundant labour and of low-cost methods of manifold increase of the productivity of assets of which the poor do dispose. In a not very indiret way, the creation of poverty has been subsidised. Poverty alleviation is neither a special topic nor a low-cost substitute for growth. Is is neither more nor less "social" than development in general. It is part of the formulation of any sustainable strategy of economic development. In the 1990s it may, and perhaps should, become the dominant issue—not as an alternative to the structural reorganisations of the 1980s, but as a means of filling a growth framework with substance.

Dr. M. Lakshmi Narasaiah

Contents

1

On the Way to Commercial Microcredits

The Changing of a Development Instrument

The founding of financial institutions in the developing countries, whose target groups are supposed to be poorer people and, in particular, income-generating micro, small-scale and medium-sized enterprises, originated in the industrialised nations. Soon after Western "development policy" began in the 1950s and 1960s the donors noted that investment in infrastructure was insufficient to achieve growth. Reflecting on the experiences of Europe, state or mixed-enterprise development banks were founded in many developing countries with the support of various donors. The banks were to promote industrialisation as a substitution for imports, as well as farming, housing construction and regional development. Their common feature was that they combined the characteristics of a bank and a public authority. On the one hand, they managed loan holdings and handled payment transactions, and on the other they "prompted" development by non-repayable grants. Since these functions each followed a very different logic, the banks were required to undertake a difficult tightrope walk.

Exclusion of Small Borrowers

As a justification for the existence of state banks, even in liberal market economies people like to point out, and rightly so, that normal commercial banks would have scarcely any interest in the business of the "small fry" and, that they also shun longer-term financing of investment. A lender cannot beforehand tell the difference between good and less good borrowers, and must set a uniform interest rate for his credit offer. In order not to lose his cost-efficient and low risk customer's, meaning to avoid what the economists call "adverse selection", he sets the interest rate not as high as he would have to in covering his costs in the case of small borrowers, and "rations" his loans according to criteria such as reputation, collateral and business volume. Even in an otherwise completely liberalised model world, small borrowers, remain excluded from formal bank loans even if they would be able and prepared to bear cost-covering terms. That applies to an even because, other being equal, in most countries of the world they have lower incomes than men and also are discriminated against in access to property rights.

Therefore, in micro-economic terms, the idea behind the founding of development banks is well-founded. However, the design of the institutional structures, including the governance structure, requires a fine balancing of the bank and public authority functions in order to reconcile efficiency, cost-covering and the promotion mission. All too often, the easy way out for all involved is to combine the negative features of bank and public authority, meaning linking profit-mongering and the exclusion of small borrowers with a subsidy mentality and polarisation. As critical studies from the 1970s showed, following the initial euphoria, development banks seldom live up to their promises.

For the donor institutions, however, these banks are ideal counterparts absorbing financial and technical assistance. Thanks to their banking function in payment transactions, they practically never have outflow problems. In addition, they can at any time produce from their broad portfolios the projects demanded by a donor or; his client, such as parliamentary committee. And promoting development banks also promotes the exports of the donors, meaning the Industrialised nations.

And important point of criticism focuses on his "hidden" promotion of exports. This is that micro, small-scale and medium-size enterprises mostly do not need a great deal of imports, and especially not so long as they are still building a trusting relationship with their bank to overcome the asymmetrical information mentioned above. So they need loans in local rather than foreign currency.

When favourably-priced foreign currency; loans are available for projects which a bank public authority or company would in any case implement or promote, these can be used for other purposes, such as for imports of consumer goods or other agreeable things which otherwise could not be afforded. So who can blame politicians, bureaucrats, bank directors or companies when they prove to be fervent supporters of the financing of development banks!

Critics of the development bank system did not have an easy task in asserting themselves against the concerted interest of individuals on both the donor and recipient sides. But the search for alternatives began on a broad front in the 1980s.

Alternatives to Development Bank Promotion

Committed politicians, bureaucrats, academics, consultants and NGOs in various countries around the world began to get down to serious work in forming a new policy. Their efforts were based on the declared principles of poverty alleviation and sustainability in intuition-building in promoting micro, small-scale and medium scale enterprises via the finance sector. The results were published in the World Bank's World Development Report of 1989.

In an initial step, so-called "integrated" rural and urban projects and programmes were equipped with their own "rotation funds". Which were to finance employment and income-generating measures. However, due to their integration in projects focussed on infrastructure measures such as slum clearance, irrigation, electrification, public health services and regional planning, they degenerated typically into drawing funds for projects management's. That meant that a recipient mentality rather than a sustainable financial service provider structure came into being, and the mixing of loans and free gifts undermined rather than promoted a positive attitude towards market-conform financial relationships.

The Grameena Bank in Bangladesh is a special case. Here, the charismatic professor Muhammed Yunus persuaded the government to place a state bank in the service of poverty alleviation, and for landless women in particular. The results are not undisputed, especially since the bank is still very dependent upon subsidies. But this institution shows that participation in the monetary economy is anything but a matter of course, and that emancipation of women as free economic citizens is a goal to which purely technological financial principles should perhaps be subordinated. The Grameen bank has yet to stand the test of developing into a sustainable institution without a heroic head and without subsides. Maybe it will really show now a poor country like Bangladesh can establish itself in the long term as a "funnel" for permanent development assistance transfers. But a final assessment does not appear to be possible at present.

The NGOs are another alternative to customary development banks. Donors like to promote them because they are close to the target groups, or at least are able to portray themselves so. In practice, however, they prove to be problematical partners when it comes to develping a durable formal finance structure in the interests of small borrowers. As committed left-wingers, NGO members and leaders usually take a skeptical stance towards the market and its "bourgeois" laws. They are seldom willing to act as bankers with all necessary toughness and assume the "ownership" of a financial institution.

Critical evaluations show that in some case NGOs can be persuaded to found financial institutions and also run them as sole or co-owners. But the success of such upgrading projects depends very much upon the consultants and donors, and above all upon the existence of a capable leader. They cannot, however, be regarded as a norm.

The target groups and the academics advising them on-site noticed after a while, of course, that the big words were hollow. They realised that first and foremost it was matter of the hidden agenda of the national and international financiers and not particularly about reducing poverty among the target groups. If the "frontier" of the formal finance sector was to be pushed downwards in the direction of the poor, what they really needed in financial services had to be made available to them. These were small, readily available operating funds and emergency loans and secure and worthwhile investment options for temporary financial surpluses. Since poverty was a mass phenomenon, these financial products had to be offered with a loan technology, meaning a form of organisation, that gave them a mass reach with as much saturation as possible.

The then prevailing pattern was "controlled investment loan", involving obligatory consultancy, subsidised interest rates and relatively large sums to push through innovations in the context of "pilot projects" which, however, due to limited subsidy funds, never got beyond the promotion of a few "pilots". So the reforms diagnosis meant a radical change. But there were enough people on either side of the political "barricades" who became convinced by this plausible if hardy grandiose concept. As a self-supporting commercial system which nevertheless was in the interests of the target groups, it began to assert itself towards the end of the 1990s under the label of "commercial approach" or "new development finance".

After the fall of the Berlin Wall

With the fading of utopic vision, empirically-based diagnoses gained ground and showed that precisely an unpretentious and reliable bank-customer relationship was the best contribution a bank could make to economic survival. In addition, they also demonstrated that in many cases a bank could in fact also help the target group of poor people, and particularly micro-and small-scale enterprises, to accumulate assets. Furthermore, it should be not only be mentioned but even emphasised that there were, and should be, public services of all kinds, including old age pensions, family allowance and similar transfers. Which counter poverty around the world. That was necessary to prevent micro credit programmes and similar bank services facing a demand they could not meet. Taking out a loan and servicing it with interest and repayment of the capital sum is always a burden for the borrower, and possible a benefit only in so far as it enable a special opportunity for profit to be sized. For the poorest of the poor, transfers are called for not loans and other bank or insurance services.

Development cooperation practicians on the ground and ideologically unbiased theorists alike came to these conclusions as early as the mid-1980s. But the ideological pressure did not ease until after the collapse of the East Bloc, when both the communist threat and the utopia of the non-capitalist workers' and farmers paradise disappeared.

So it is not surprising that shortly afterwards the patricians of both sides and the immediate representatives of the target groups got together with enlightened representatives of donors, consultants and academics to form an international coalition titled "New Development Finance". The Microcredit Summit of 1997 with Hillary Clinton and already leaned in this direction, even if it still sent no clear signal in regard to the issue of dependency on subsidies. But the donors gave a green light for a massive financial promotion. World Bank president James Wolfensohn promised that together with all the other summit participants he would go all to ensure that by 2005 an additional 100 million families around the world would have microcredits.

The subsequent "Annual Conferences on New Development Finance", which took place at the University of Frankfurt - Main from 1997 to 1999, then developed into an important forum at which formerly diametrically opposed actors joined forces against the "ancient regime", According to their definition, "old" is everything which boils down to the demand of re-educating people and coupling loans with obligatory consultancy. In the long term, that results in dependency on subsidies, becoming hostage to the political games of influential national rulers and donors, and loses sight of the declared target group of the urban and rural poor. All this applies mainly to smaller countries which receive heavy international assistance. In India, Pakistan and Brazil, not to mention China, the conditions have their own rhythms and special features.

After the end of communism there was a new situation not only in the developing countries and the North-South relationship, but also and above all in Eastern Europe. Established donor institutions such as USAID and the Reconstruction Loan Corporate (KfW) were supplemented by the multilateral European Bank for Reconstruction and Development (EBRD), and what were soon to be called "transformation Countries" lined up with the "classic" recipients of international development aid.

Internationally operating NGOs and consultancies with experience if the microcredit systems of developing countries were not also called for to assist the projects and programmes in Eastern Europe. The finance sector was perceived as the core of every market economy. At the same time, the donors soon recognised the importance of small to medium-sized business, trades, small holders and all the many disparate micro and small-scale enterprises for employment and the supply of the population. However, financial services were not available to any great degree to cover their needs.

It could now be seen that payment transactions did not function without commercial banks, and that this shortcoming and a considerable negative impact on small enterprises. Going beyond microcredits, which until then had always been the main instrument of financial assistance, the focus was now on deposits, transfers and all the other financial services that were important for the target groups. "Micro financing" gradually became the generic term for the orientation of financial sector measures to benefit the "small people".

Downscaling" or "Starting from Scratch"

By means of special loan programmes, which were kept separate from the other portfolios, the external donors sought at first to persuade the existing banks to downscale their activities and address the newly emerging small to medium-size business in the private sector. On balance, the result was rather meager, for these programmes did little to influence the characteristics of the major Eastern European commercial banks. And every time some of them were privatised or had to be shut down due to financial rows or corruption scandals, it affected the special small enterprises portfolios regardless of how efficiently they were managed.

Besides using this channel via the big banks, donors also began building up loan programmes through NGOs and local chambers of commerce. The result here were also disappointing, for local implementing organisations are mostly unsuitable for a substantial mass banking business.

But senior officials and executive at donors and consultancies soon had the idea of founding their own micro-finance institutes. "Starting from scratch" green field banking and similar terms began to make the rounds The first "Micro-Enterprises Bank" came into being in Bosnia and soon afterwards other micro-finance institutions (MFIs) were founded.

Unlike customary development cooperation projects, which have a timeframe, the MFIs are open-ended, and consultants in the North also see themselves as long-term partner. In contrast, international development organisations are more and more becoming second-class partners from which local bodies must sooner or later separate themselves again to avoid being left in the lurch. After all, their cooperation has a time limit, and they will leave the country again.

In view of the challenges of globalisation, the banks should perhaps consider using their development projects to establish a network of long term investments and thus fulfil their promotion mission in favour of the "Small people" not only locally and nationally, but also globally.

2

Small People's Banks

The Role of Micro-Enterprise Banks in Development Assistance

Micro-enterprise banks (MEBs) grant many small loans, offer investment opportunities, and handle their customer's payment transactions at home and abroad. They are licensed by and under the control of local banking supervisory bodies. They are growing fast and expanding their branch networks.

Direct observation and simple arithmetics show that the banks make a substantial contribution to local finance systems and thus to their countries' economic development. Their input to development is socially relevant above all because they offer their services first and foremost to the kinds of customers in which existing local banks appear to have a no interest. Apart from the jobs in the small enterprises they finance, the banks themselves offer many young people skilled employment. In addition, these small banks make a profit. They also have private investors, who are becoming more and more important to them.

All that appears to be quite astonishing, most of all perhaps because MEB are founded as development assistance projects. A consensus has emerged in development cooperation in recent years in which institutions such as MEB appear to be a new model. The MEBs are the newcomers on this list, and their success can already be noted from their figures. A more precise analysis seeking to isolate the quantitative influence of their various success factors, including that of donor inputs, would require more data than is available due to the newness of the MEBs. But what already appears to be clear is that establishing new banks is a promising new approach in the microfinance sector.

Learning from Experience

The new approach is an attempt to draw lessons from the positive and negative experiences of financing development and implement them. An initial and very positive lesson relates to the methods of granting loans. It is indeed possible to grant, with tolerable costs and a very low repayment default rate, microcredits to people whom conventional bankers view as a not creditworthy and in whom established banks have no interest.

This methodology is neither a secret nor difficult to learn. However, it is not compatible with the organisational structures and processes of customary banks, which are focussed on other business fields and target groups. That is the second lesson, drawn from many so-called downscaling projects. To be successful at granting small-scale and micro-loans, a bank must be capable and willing to go in for far-reaching decentralisation of decision-making agree to performance related pay, and offer skilled employees credible job and promotion prospects. And to achieve that the bank must also grow. As a counterbalance to decentralisation bank staff must be very well trained and highly motivated, and sophisticated control mechanisms must be in place.

These considerations are good reasons for offering financial services for "small" people through special institutions. This was attempted in the past by the strategy of upgrading existing loan granting NGOs by external support. The experiences with upgrading were in part very good, but some of them were problematical.

The third lesson is clearly positive. It is indeed possible, with acceptable expenditure of development assistance funds to upg-ade on existing institution and transform if into an efficient bank for "small customers. And that brings us to the fourth and rather negative lesson. Upgrading as inherent has inherent limits. Positions based on power and self-interest arise in the process of developing and promoting existing institutions, and they obstruct a project's progress. The manager or founder/initiator of an externally promoted and relatively successful loan-granting NGO naturally has little interest in his or her institution becoming a "proper bank" for whose management they would not be suitable, if due only to the banking supervisory body's qualification requirements. The donors, too, who usually have financed the expansive first stage of an upgrading process, regrettably often do not see themselves as owners and advocates of the promoted institutions and, above all, of the target groups they have not yet reached. As a rule they are satisfied with what has been achieved. They avoid a confrontation with those who defend their positions and thereby impede further development of the institution, even if this is desirable in development terms.

It is precisely successful institution—strengthening that aggravates the dichotomy between those who have attained influential and prestigious positions and want to protect their interests and the interests of the target groups and the bank's employees in expanding the institution. This conflict, for which there is plenty of empirical proof, has a structural cause. NGOs have no owners that have an "objective" interest in the long-term financial and developmental success of the projects and will therefore assume a constructive role. Formalising the institution changes so long as there is not at the same time a substantial change in the ownership structure.

Setting up New Microfinance Banks

The new approach differs in two respects from customary institution building by upgrading. First, the phases of institution strengthening ahead of formalising and transforming are leapfrogged. Instead of expanding and converting an NGO, it is about setting up a new micro finance bank. Second, the issue of ownership and governance are clarified from the start based on the perspective of medium-term development. But the more technical problems of granting loans and the design of the institution can be solved largely according to proven models.

Setting up a bank from scratch in a developing or transformation country involves a number of steps. The first is project identification. The main question here is whether the project could make developmental sense. The second step is to assess whether a new bank is really necessary and meaningful in developmental terms, economically sound and politically feasible, Economic soundness is assessed under the assumption that for the initial phase technical assistance and refinancing of the first loans on favourable terms can be procured. Without these, the projects could not be implemented at precisely the time when they appeared to be particularly important for development.

In the third step, provisional consensus must be reached among potential investors and the so-called sponsor, who is to build up the bank in technical terms and manage it during its early days. In addition, knock-on financing from one or more donors must be secured. What is decisive for potential inclusion as an international investor is first to be willing and able to play an active role as a an owner and be present on the board of the new bank. The second requirement is to contribute to the success of the project above and beyond having a capital stake in it. The third condition is to share the concept of a commercially oriented strategy of institution building that is nevertheless committed to development.

The second condition can be fulfilled by, for example, an investor also functioning as a donor and providing Technical Cooperation funds or loans or procuring them from pure donors. If the other two conditions were not met, coordination would be too difficult. The group of possible investors who fulfill as the perquisites is very limited. Investors who had only capital to offer would be quite easy to find. But including them in the setting-up phase would only hamper coordination. In principle, the development institutions are possible project sponsors, who should also be investors. But in practice there is more a tendency to call in a private company with relevant experience.

The fourth step is to develop a business plan. This forms the basis for a biding commitment by the investors, the sponsors and, if applicable, the donors. The plan also covers the founding of a local company as the legal entity responsible for the future bank, the application for bank licence, and the technical preparation for opening the bank including recruiting and training local staff.

If the entire process is completed quickly, it takes a year. Based on experienced, compared with upgrading projects the time needed for setting up a functioning bank is shorter, the cost to donors lower and the chances of success greater.

Success Depends on Natural Trust and Experience

The success of the new Banks promotes their employee's commitment and loyalty and strengthens the link between investors and sponsors. It thereby reinforce precisely the factors that are required of them to allow this success to occur. That is why time and gain the same actors get together in various projects as international investors, sponsors and donors. All parties must know each other well and have well-founded trust in each other for last and successful handling of the process. And only a rapid sequence of similar projects involving the same actors officers the opportunity of transferring knowledge, including qualified staff, from one "building site" to the next. Where if not in similar projects, can someone who is to set up and manage a microfinacne bank or their loans department learn how to do it? Where, other than in a "sister" project, is local staff to be trained before the bank is opened? Where, other than in similar and effectively linked banks, are there the opportunities of advancement, which must be offered, to the best local staff in order to strengthen their motivation and retain them?

3

After the Mocrocredit Sumit

How to Implement Its Anti-Poverty Strategy

More than 2500 people from 100 countries gathered in Washington in February, 1997, to participate in the Microcredit Summit. The goal of the organisers of the Summit is to reach 100 million poor families around the world with microcredits and other financial services within the next ten years. As there are at least six people in a family, 600 million people would benefit from access to micro finance. This means that half of the people in extreme poverty could have the opportunity to get out of their misery.

The fact that more than one billion people in the world are still living in extreme poverty is a sign of failure of our development policy and a scandal for human society. Now there is no longer any excuse. We have learned in the last years that microcredit is one of the best tools to eradicate poverty. At the Summit, there was a consensus between politicians, practitioners, donors, scientists and NGOs on how to reach this goal. Particular emphasis is given to strengthening poor people in their capacities. It is also understood that lack of funds is only one aspect of the most pressing problems in the field of micro finance.

The Approach

The overall goal can be achieved by designing and establishing an appropriate and sustainable institutional framework on the national level in the developing countries.

The most significant elements within a feasible strategy to achieve the goal are the following:

- Decentralised, bilateral fund-raising and financing under commonly accepted standards are preferred, whereas the creation of a new global facility as a supranational mobilising and channeling mechanism for micro credit should not be pursued.
- The focal point of the future strategy should be the creation and the support of independent and recipient countries which will operate under the basic principles of outreach. Moreover, the mobilisation of domestic funds will be of particular importance. Promoting agencies as wholesale institutions should identify and assess eligible microfinance institutions on the basis of a widely accepted set of performance criteria, identify institutional weakness and requirements at national level and execute programmes for the funding, institutional strengthening, training and linking of participating institutions.
- The NGO Results, which helped organise the Microcredit Summit, will perform as a catalyst in creating public awareness regarding the crucial role of microfinance in poverty alleviation in donor as well as recipient countries.

The Consultative Group to Assist the Poorest (CGAP) will be responsible for the creation of promoting agencies at the national level. The role of CGAP will be the monitoring and coordinating of promotional activities. It will act as a platform for setting consistent standards for the operation of individual programmes.

The Next Steps

Under the guidance of CGAP, interested donor and recipient countries should immediately begin to discuss the institutional profiles of promoting agencies and performance criteria of participating institutions. Moreover, the necessary operational procedures for the functioning of the institutional framework at the wholesale level need to be defined by CGAP. CGAP should identify promoting agencies within the next six months. It will be responsible for the coordination of funding activities. Capacity building for promoting agencies as well as for recipient institutions will be a crucial issue. A pilot phase in a small number of countries should be designed to gain experience with the proposed institutional framework in order to develop it further and also determine the adequate volume of funding for potential recipient institutions. Bilateral donors should support these activities.

The Role of Financial Markets and the IMF

The Genesis of Asia's Financial Crisis

It is obvious that the major causes of Asia's financial crisis were rooted in the affected countries. The evils were excessive foreign borrowing, poor supervision of banks, and overvaluation of national currencies. Apart from those policy failures, however, there were external factors. These were, besides the instability of the international finance markets, above all the wrong reaction of the International Monetary Fund, which aggravated the crisis rather than counteracting it. The role of the IMF must be fundamentally redefined.

The Asian crisis marks for the time being the end of the Southeast and East Asian economic miracle of the last four decades. Engulfed by the malaise of the worst-hit countries, Thailand, Indonesia and South Korea, the entire region in suffering economic weakness and in part even a decline in economic performance. The question is whether the Asian crisis could have been avoided or whether wrong economic policy decisions gave it a kick-start.

The Causes of the Crisis

Analysis of the causes for the Asian crisis have to date been marked by an astonishing one-sidedness. Up front, explanations emphasise the internal causes, particularly the private sector's excessive foreign borrowing. But two other factors played central, if not decisive, roles in the spread of the crisis. One was the great Volatility of the international capital markets, the other the inappropriate policies of the IMF.

This article analysis these three major causes of the crisis. Another question is how in future one can prevent manageable economic problems getting out of hand and developing into a crisis that threatens more than the economic stability of single countries.

But a closer look shows that the crisis, which broke out in mid-1997, has assumed such an unforeseen dimension that individual corrective measures of economic policy can no longer cope with it. A huge structural economic crisis has arisen. What developments led to it ?

Foreign Borrowing

Let us look first at the high private sector borrowing abroad. With hindsight, it is easy to pass judgement on it as having been wrong and dangerous. But that does not mean that private foreign borrowing is harmful in general. If it finances profitable investments, it is merely the use of foreign savings when domestic savings are too low. IMF reports also reflected this assessment.

We know from experience of earlier debt crisis that a high foreign indebtedness by the private sector is latently, but not generally, risky. The Asian crisis also has reconfirmed that international finance markets differentiate between individual private debtors and the credit-worthiness of national economies only in the case of a few countries. In smaller countries, including OECD member South Korea, difficulties in servicing individual loans lead to investors getting out of these markets. This is the real danger of large-scale private foreign debts.

That makes foreign loans much more expensive than domestic credits. If the national interest rate is higher than that of international market, cash deposit requirement often can be an adequate incentive to borrow at home or take out a longer-term loan. Both alternatives lead to greater stability of the domestic finance system, as the risk of withdrawal of capital at short notice, as in the case of the Asian crisis countries, is much reduced.

Instability of the Finance Markets

Beyond the cash deposit requirement, however, further restructuring must be done in the finance sectors of the Asian crisis economies and threshold and developing countries. Frequently, the are demands for greater transparency. Improved banking supervision and, especially in the case of South Korea, a broader diversification of shareholding. These steps are important, but they will not prevent the next crisis because they do not put an end to the instability of the international finance markets.

The Asian crisis has also reconfirmed that highly mobile capital can produce instability. It must seem dubious when there are calls (particularly by the IMF and US politicians involved in financial matters) for the pushing through of even more capital mobility as a consequence of the crisis. But even liberal economists are now increasingly questioning the ideal of a world without restrictions on the free movement of capital linked with an enhanced IMF mandate.

IMF Intervention

The IMF's policy intensified the volatility of the international capital flows, that is, their wide fluctuation margin. When American and European fund managers began to pull their capital out of Asia's crisis countries, Asian debtors fell into arrears in servicing their liabilities, and the currencies came under heavy pressure, the IMF ordered a drastic cure. This was aimed at lowering inflation rates and reducing government budget deficits. But as there were not critical inflaction rates, and government budgets were in fact, in surplus, this policy was more than odd. A quick look at the economic development in the Asian crisis countries illustrates the relatively positive situation of the three economies before the crisis broke out.

What Measures to Stabilise Currencies?

The IMF policy also manifests deficiencies beyond the measures it ordered. I shall not discuss here the question of whether it is wise and appropriate for the IMF to clamp measures and restrictions of private sector debtors and their governments while the creditors side can emerge from the crisis largely without loss.

But one must ask whether the IMF's measures to stabilise the currencies were suitable in an acute-crisis. They are mainly measures with individual impacts, giving priority to increasing real interest rates. The aim is to regain the trust of international finance markets and stimulate fresh loan flows to these countries. The long-term objective is to restore currency stability.

This policy, however, has to weaknesses. On the one hand, it sets indebted companies under more pressure as they must not only pay more for their foreign currency loans due to devaluation, but are also faced with higher domestic interest. On the other hand, while it is true that a high interest rate policy in countries with stable economies can have a positive impact in attracting capital, that is not so in countries suffering from an acute economic crisis, as Indonesia shows. Recovery of the exchange rate to a realistic level that would enable the companies to service their debts has not happened there.

The Future of the IMF

Having reflected upon the dubious results of the IMF policy, one is bound to ask what role the organisation should play in future. Should its task be to have a stabilising effect in a crisis, or should the IMF be an instrument to assert certain economic policy concepts?

The IMF itself has defined its current function very one-sidedly, focussing on its services for the international finance markets. According to a self-assessment in an internal IMF document, it sees itself performing a dual function as a 'confidental economic adviser' and as the 'watchdog for the international financial markets'. But the IMF does not by a long way give the attention they deserve to the interests of the 350 million people in the countries under its wing.

Criticism in the West

Criticism of the IMF is growing not only in the Asian crisis countries but also especially in the USA and more and more in Europe. Conservative American politicians such as the former US Secretary of State Charles Shultz have described the IMF as ineffective, unnecessary and obsolute. They have also proposed that the IMF be abolished at some time after the Asian crisis has been overcome. The IMF's current policy is also coming in for heavy criticism in the academic debate on the crisis, which is demanding a redefinition of the organisation's mandate.

Other possibilities are conceivable beyond the radical option of abolishing or privatising the IMF. The IMF should in any case be required to tackle the specific situations in the crisis countries with greater awareness of the affected countries. In the course of the Asian crisis, the option of creating a regional fund was also discussed, but the Western G7 countries and the IMF emphatically rejected it. One should, however, consider whether regional institutions could not in fact work more efficiently than an authority based in Washington with competence for the entire world.

A regional structure with several monetary funds could facilitate the overcoming of crisis situations, although only if a global structure were to be maintained alongside the regional components. This global body, a kind of world monetary council, would be composed of representatives of the US and European central banks and the regional funds. Besides taking over the IMF's current tasks, such an international regime could also deal with stabilising exchange rates between the industrialised nations and in particular with the development of a target zones system between the dollar and the Euro. The winners in a less unstable international finance system would be the developing and threshold countries that at present still need to take the questionable medicine prescribed by the IMF.

5

The Status of Saving

National savings rates have been declining for several years in many countries of the industrial and developing world. Given the importance of saving to the global economy, this trends is causing much concern. Saving is critical to maintain growth and to help solve the problem of international debt. Declining saving rates have been associated with lower rates of capital accumulation and slower growth in the global economy. Moreover, differing rates of saving among countries have contributed to the emergence of large trade imbalances.

Most economies agree that if these long-run trends continue, they would have a serious impact on international economic growth. Yet attention has recently shifted to the potential consequences of a more immediate threat—that of a short-run global capital shortage. There are claims that this is caused by increase demands on global financial resources resulting from such events as the process of transition in Eastern Europe and the former Soviet Union, German unification, reconstruction of the Middle East, disaster relief, and structural support of countries in debt. At the same time, large private and public sector deficits persist in important industrial countries. Even countries like Germany and Japan are experiencing a decline in their traditional surpluses of capital because of structural changes in their economies.

These factors mean that world capital markets are likely to become increasingly competitive. Countries needing capital in both North and South may face scarcer supplies of funds.

Can the perceived shortage of global savings be avoided? Do the world's financial markets have the capacity to absorb additional demands for funds? Can structural changes in the global economy take place in the global economy take place in a way that does not jeopardize growth? Or, will a savings shortage perpetuate high interest rates (or even increase them) and limit economic growth?

Trends in Saving

Global savings and investment are notoriously difficult to measure. The latest reliable estimate puts total world saving at approximately US $5.2 Trillion in 1995. On a global scale, both saving and investment have declined as a percentage of the gross national product (GNP) since the early 1980s.

Since the mid-1980s, the OECD countries have become net importers of capital. Al over the world, and particularly in North America and a few other industrial countries, government debt generates a demand for money. OPEC countries provided most of the financial resources needed by world markets during the 1980s. But since the downturn in oil prices hit the OPEC region in 1983s, newly industrializsing countries in Asia (and particularly Taiwan) have largely take over this role. About 80 per cent of total private saving is accumulated in the industrial world. In the developing world, Africa has consistently suffered from insufficient saving, although the situation has improved slightly during the 1980s. More recently, Asian and Latin American countries have become excess savers.

Global Balance

For an individual country, or even a region, imbalances between savings and investment are not necessarily critical. A country can invest more than it saves and borrow what it needs on capital markets. Countries that are excess savers supply the necessary funds. On a global scale, however, the supply of savings must equal the demand for investment. In other words, one country's investment must be another country's savings.

But the global balance between planned saving and desired investment can be lopsided. For example, grater demands for investment will trigger processes of adjustment; either the price of borrowing capital will rise (i.e., higher interest rates) or certain investment projects will not be funded. Capital shortages largely affect world markets through higher interest rates. Indeed, world interests rates did rise during the 1980s and the early 1990s. The 1980s have in fact been quite atypical, in that real (meaning corrected for inflation) interest rates have persisted at unprecedented levels. Possibly as a result of greater demands on world financial markets. Competing economic theories have identified a number of potential culprits for this enduring increase. An insufficient amount of savings (either current or expected) is only one of many hypotheses explaining the rise in real interest rates.

Reduced Demand

The unification of Germany, the transitional economies of Eastern Europe and the Commonwealth of Independent States, reconstruction of the Middle East, and new lending to developing countries account for about a 3 per cent increase in demand for world savings. There are, however, trends in other areas that appear to signal a reduced need for funds. For example, investment has slowed in the previously booming commercial real estate markets in the United States and elsewhere. Moreover, there are indications that the rates of fixed investment in Japan during the 1980s are not likely to be sustained.

The possibility also exists for more savings in the public sector industrial countries. These range from prospects for tax increases in Germany to massive reductions in military expenditures, particularly in the US. The rapid advancement of European integration is likely to lead to improved fiscal discipline and consolidated budgets, and thus reduced public sector spending. At any rate, government deficits are still critical and reducing them will be important for future national saving in industrial countries.

Private saving behaviour is difficult to project in that it reflects as society's values and changing preferences. The latest medium-term International Monetary Fund forecast, however, show that private savings in industrial countries will drop by about 0.5 per cent of GNP, primarily because of a rapidly aging population and the corresponding increase in the ratio of dependents to wage earners in Japan and many European countries.

Although world saving might be insufficient over the short-and medium-term, it is also evident that even small changes in the current economic environment and in public and private sector behaviour could generate enough funds to eliminate the problem entirely. A first conclusion is, therefore, that forecasts of a major saving gap or an imminent capital shortfall should be treated with some sceptism. Consequently, concerns that insufficient saving will lead to increases in world real interest rates are also mostly unwarranted.

Credit Squeeze

Claims on world financial resources are likely to squeeze the amount of capital available from multilateral development banks and bilateral institutions to many small developing countries. This rationing of financial support may be as important for this group of countries as the potential eroding of the favourable terms of international lending. Small adjustments to the level of support can translate into significant setbacks for the most vulnerable countries.

Any globally co-ordinate scheme to give financial aid to selected regions must include safeguards so that the smallest, least developed, and highly indebted countries still have access to the finite sources of capital available to international agencies.

Why should individual countries be concerned about the global supply of funds, when, in the long run, growth for any country is financed out of domestic saving? There is little evidence to suggest that the degree of access to external funds effects medium-term growth rates in developing countries. In fact, during the last two decades, economic growth was generally lower in the developing countries that borrowed than in those that did not. This was largely due to the high interest rates of the 1980s suffered by severely indebted countries. Even earlier, however, borrowers' growth rates were only marginally higher than those of non-borrowers. Although the borrowed funds helped boost per-capita income, it is less likely that they stimulated the economies of the recipient countries. Differences in the developing countries' growth have largely been the result of differences in their rates of domestic saving. Form this perspective, national saving should be encouraged.

Fears Unfounded

A tentative conclusion is that fears or a global capital shortage, skyrocketing real interest rates, and negative effects resulting from greater demands on international financial resources over the next few years are most likely unfounded. There appears to be as many trends pointing toward increases in saving as there are indications of additional capital needs. Also, even if substantial savings shortfalls were to materialise, the limited rise in real interest rates would have relatively benign effects on countries of both North and South. The only major caveat relates to small developing countries that have in the past depended upon favourable terms of lending from multi-and bilateral institutions. If international capital shortages translate into even the smallest encroachment on the allocation of funds to these countries, their medium-term development could be threatened. In addition, the debt burdens of many developing countries suggest that in the long-run, external sources of funds cannot substitute for sufficient national saving. If domestic saving correspondents to development needs in the

South, developing countries should not suffer as a result of increased competition for international capital.

Finally, while the short-term fears of a global capital shortage are clearly unwarranted, concerns about the medium-term trends in world saving are not. National saving rates must be raised substantially throughout the world to allow real interest rates to decline to the post-war average of 1 to 1.5 per cent. That, more than anything else, will contribute to a stable expansion of the global economy.

6

Finance Matters

Financial Liberalisation Too Much too Soon?

An efficient and stable financial system is important for economic growth and poverty reduction,. The financial crises that have afflicted many countries in recent times have been a costly and painful reminder of the disastrous consequences for development of weak financial markets. The recurrence of financial crises, at both the international and national levels, and the adverse effect they have had on economic growth and poverty levels, have highlighted the need for a policy framework which addresses the inherent vulnerability of financial markets to systemic instability and failure.

Governments have always intervened in the financial sector and there are sound theoretical and practical reasons for doing so. Financial markets are characterised by problems of limited and unequal information, making them inherently imperfect and prone to failure. Financial regulation and supervision are therefore essential for efficient and stable financial market development. How should governments intervene? Have financial liberalisation and financial sector reform made financial systems more, or less vulnerable to instability and systemic crises? How can the process be better managed? What is the best policy framework for supporting financial sector development in low-income countries.

Repression to Liberalisation

For many years, governments followed a policy of financial 'repression', which relied on fixing interest rates below market levels and controlling the allocation of credit. The economic distortions induced by these policies were considerable. Financial systems remained under-developed, lending patterns were inefficient and failed to achieve their distributional goals. Negative real interest rates led to low savings and encouraged capital flight. Macro-economic performance also deteriorated countries with large negative real interest rates experienced lower location efficiency and growth rates. In the state owned banking sector, poor lending decisions (often politically influenced) and low repayment rates led to bank insolvency and large budgetary bailouts of depositors and creditors.

A growing awareness of the economic costs of financial 'repression', led to financial 'liberalisation' as the dominant policy paradigm over the past two decades. Initially, the relaxation of controls on interest rates was the focus for financial reform which was often triggered by a financial crisis. The relaxation of controls on the financial sector was often part of a more general policy shift towards liberalisation of the domestic economy and opening out the international economy liberalisation soon broadened therefore beyond interest rate liberalisation, to include a wide range of measures constituting a programme of financial sector reform was adopted under World bank sectoral or structural adjustment lending conditionalities, the key elements of which included privatisation of banks, entry of new domestic and foreign entrants in to the banking sector, bank restructuring and recapitalisation, opening upto the capital account, strengthening bank regulation and supervision institutions.

Has Financial Liberalisation Worked

The period of financial liberalisation conincided with, or was soon followed by heightened financial instability, culminating in the dramatic financial crisis in East Asia in the second half of the 1990s. Clearly, financial liberalisation has not led to a smooth transition to a stable and efficient financial system. It would be wrong, however, to jump to the easy, but shallow, conclusion that financial liberalisation has 'failed'. Firstly, the fat that the period of increased systemic instability does not prove causality. Secondly, no process of change comes cheap: a reasoned assessment of the costs and benefits of the policy changes is needed. And thirdly, what would have been the outcome without the policy change" Finally the impact of financial liberalisation will differ between countries, depending on each country's economic and institutional characteristics. The more relevant research issue, therefore, relates to the design and timing of context-specific policy measures, which will contribute to the development of an efficient and stable financial system. Could financial liberalisation have been managed better? If so, what policies are now needed? The commercial banks are the dominant component of the financial sector in low-income countries and are critical to the efficiency and stability of the financial system as a whole. Financial liberalisation was associated with a shift in prudential regulation from direct regulation of banks, by for example, regular site visits, to an indirect approach based on the monitoring of bank capital to ensure that it remained adequate in relation to the risk being taken. Additional regulatory measures are also necessary to restrain the activities of the privitised and other newly-established private banks. The regulatory and supervisory framework may also need to be extended, to cover micro-finance institutions which have developed significant deposit taking capacity.

Four main obstacles to efficient banking regulations are:

(a) information, contracting and monitoring problems;

(b) Lack of supervisory personnel;

(c) High operational costs; and

(d) Poor credibility and regulation of regulatory bodies. The appropriateness of various policy measures for dealing with these constraints are discussed and ranked in

terms of their suitability for low-income countries. What are the implications of allowing micro-finance institutions to offer a range of financing services beyond small-scale lending.

Too Much, Too Soon?

The experience with financial liberalisation reveals a strong correlation between liberalisation and financial crisis. This can be explained partly by the exposure of existing inefficiencies and distortions in the financial structure, and partly by a failure to develop a strong regulatory and supervisory framework, prior to liberalisation. Weakness in the initial conditions affect the ability of the privatised banks and new market entrants, to operate on broadly commercial principles. Borrowers are often unable to service their loans, due to poor quality lending and high interest rates. Liberalisation of the capital account increases the inflow of foreign capital, but at the same time threatens that stability of the financial institutions by increasing the exchange rate and domestic lending risks.

The existing regulatory and supervisory system may be unsuited to a market-based environment. Consequently, across-the-broad 'big-bang' financial liberalisation and financial sector reform increase the likelihood of systemic crisis, where the institutional and human resource environment is weak. Much of the blame for post-liberalisation financial crisis lies, therefore, with the scale and sequencing of financial reform. What is needed is a more gradual and considered approach to financial liberalisation, which recognises that institutional strengthening, especially in the regulation and supervision capacity, is a prerequisite and supervision capacity is a prerequisite for creating a more efficient and stable financial sector which can contribute fully to achieving economic growth and poverty reduction in developing countries.

7

Tobin Tax

James Tobin, a Nobel laureate in economics, dreamt up his idea for a 'Tobin tax' in the 1960s when the gold exchange standard was still in force. Before long the US closed the gold window' at the Federal Reserve, giving rise to the current regime of floating currencies. Tobin argued that speculative flows of 'hot money' would put unwanted pressure on fixed exchange rates not reflecting economic fundamentals, and would upset macro-economic management he thought that if purchases and sales of foreign currency were subject to a small tax (a fraction of 1% of the value of each transaction), long-term investment and current account operations would not be significantly affected, but currency speculators conducting large volumes of transactions adding upto a high value would be deterred.

The Tobin tax has never been implemented and was largely forgotten until in the mid 1990s. The late Mahbut ul haq and his fellow authors of the United Nations Development Programme's annual Human Development Report then received the idea with a view not so much to claming fever in the international capital market as rising extra resources to finance development. Now, War on Want is echoing this call in its report Costing the Casino: The Real impact of Currency Speculation in the 1990s.

Currency speculation plays a central role in global instability which in turn brings increased poverty and instability to developing countries, argues War on want. Its report shows, for example, that the delayed effects of the South East Asia economic crisis in 1997/98 countries to hit the poor.

At a time of declining official flows, developing countries rely more and more on private capital flows to finance their growth. Their dependence on volatile, short-term investment exposes their fragile economies to sudden changes in financial markets. The frequency of financial crises around the world in itself urges measures to stabilise this volatility.

A Tobin tax could help deter speculation by making currency trading more costly, in particular it would act to deter short-term transactions of large sums between countries more expansive.

Another advantage of the tax, says War on Want, is its revenue-rising potential-particularly in view of the 'current diminishing scale of aid budgets'. The organisation believes the threat of further economic crisis, as in South East Asia, makes the adoption—or at least consideration—of a Tobin tax 'matter of some urgency'.

However its critics say the Tobin Tax rises a number of thorny questions: Does it make economic sense? The consensus view of economists is that markets, including capital markets, work best if information is good, transaction costs are minimised and distractions removed. The Tobin tax would introduce an, albeit small, transaction cost and distraction. True capital markets are subject to bubbles and panics. But taxes are not the way to deal with these. Instead, three needs to be better supervision of markets and institutions, with occasional official (or IMF) intervention to preserve stability?

Would the Tobin tax work? If applied, it would almost certainly be subject to massive avoidance as tax-liable transactions were relocated in financial centers whose authorities had not agreed to implement the tax. There are no internationally-recognised means of obliging countries to raise a tax. Furthermore, there is a very rapidly increasing volume of transactions in foreign exchange derivatives-futures, options and swaps. It is not clear if these would be taxed also.

Would the tax raise significant resources for development? Very large sums could theoretically be raised if foreign exchange markets all applied the tax and if there were no avoidance, and if the governments which collected the tax were willing to devoted the proceeds to aid. But governments have no overriding reason to hypothecate the revenue from any particular source to aid (why not devote the proceeds of airport departure tax to aid?).

According to its critics, the Tobin Tax was not a very good idea for achieving its original purpose of claming speculations, for both theoretical and practical reasons. Nor is it a good idea as a source of more aid for the same practical reasons (is it workable?).Even if these were overcome it would require the assent and collaboration of the very governments whose current decisions to provide aid (or not) hitherto determined the magnitude of aid flows.

8

Third World Debt is Still Growing

Developing country debt is estimated to have grown to over $ 1.8 trillion last year, up from $1.77 trillion in 1994. During the past decade, much of this debt has been restructured-renegotiated on terms more favourable to debtor countries. Some 80 per cent of the funds owed to commercial banks, as well as a much smaller share of loans from governments and multilateral institutions, have now been restructured. The trend has led some analysts to declare the debt crisis over, at least for the private banks. But the poorest nations have yet to see much relief. Their debt service payments still eat up a substantial percentage of their export revenues—some 15 to 19 per cent, depending upon the measurements used. Thc ratio typical of the era before the crisis began in 1982 was on the order of 10 to 12 per cent.

The worst debt today is that of sub-Saharan Africa, excluding South Africa. Collectively the region's debt amounts to $ 180 billion, three times the 1980 total, and 10 per cent higher than its entire output of goods and services. Debt service payments come to $10 billion annually, about four times what the region spends on health and education combined. The burden is choking off economic development over much of the continent.

Eastern Europe and the countries of the former Soviet Union are also heavily indebted, but the picture varies considerably from one country to another. The region's total debt rose from 161 per cent of export earnings in 1986 to an estimated 291 per cent last year. Russia owes over $80 billion, and the country is hard pressed to meet its obligations: interest payments in 1994 were budgeted at less than 15 per cent of interest due. Poland, on the other hand, had 40 per cent of its debt forgiven in a restructuring agreement last year. Half of Bulgaria's debt was forgiven in 1993.

In Latin America, restructuring has eased the burdens of three major borrowers—Mexico, Argentina, and Brazil. Peru is the region's last remaining country with significant unrestructured debt. Peru's debt currently amounts to $26 billion.

Restructuring has brought some new actors onto the scene—and changed the roles of established players. After shedding much of the "old", high-risk debt of the 1980s, the commercial banks are moving aggressively into lucrative east Asian markets, and into private sector lending in Latin America. This more selective lending has allowed American banks, for instance, to post a 17 per cent increase in Third World loans over the year ending last March, and a 33 per cent increase since 1990.

As private lending goes elsewhere, the poorest countries have had to rely increasingly on multilateral institutions like the World Bank and the International Monetary Fund. Multilateral debt among the lowest income countries grew from around 15 per cent of total debt in 1980s to over 24 per cent in 1992. Multilateral loans generally come with much stricter terms. Neither the World Bank nor the IMF will directly forgive or restructure debt, since that might jeopardise their "preferred status" in capital markets and force them to raise interest rates. Their preferred status also means that payments to these institutions take precedence over payments to all other creditors. Of the various types of external debt, multilateral loans generally have the most rigid terms.

The multilaterals do, however, participate in a form of restructuring by providing most of the financing for "Brady" bonds, used to restructure the old debt of "middle income" countries like Brazil, Mexico, and Argentina. But the bonds are not available to the poorest countries.

Organisations that aren't in the business of lending money have become involved in restructuring as well, through swap agreements. Debt swaps reduce the amount owed in return for some concession on the part of the debtor. In debt-for-equity swaps, for example, a corporation purchases a debtor nation's IOU from a bank, and then trades it for one of the country's state-owned assets, such as a steel mill or a telephone company Debt-or equity swaps are often part of a larger privatisation strategy, especially in Latin America. While privatisation may often be necessary for saving nationalised industries, many observers are concerned that indebtedness is forcing countries to part with their assets at "fire sale" prices. Between 1985 and 1992, debt-for-equity swaps accounted for nearly 36 per cent of all debt conversions.

Debt-for-nature and debt-for-development swaps are intended to win government commitments to environmental and development projects. In these arrangements, a non-governmental organisation (NGO) usually obtains the debtor nation's IOU from a bank at a significant discount. The NGO then typically restructures the debt by passing along some of the discount conceded by the bank, accepting payments in local currency, and investing the returns locally, to fund a national part, for instance, or a public health project. Between 1985 and 1992, these types of swaps accounted for only about 2 per cent of debt conversions. But for some countries, they may already be offering significant relief: Madagascar has cut its $100 million commercial bank debt in half through debt-for-nature swaps.

9

Revisiting Bretton Woods

Reforming the World Trade and Finance System

That leading trio of major multilateral economic institutions (the International Monetary Fund and World Bank in Washington D.C. and the WTO in Geneva) were created from the ashes of World War Two to build a strong, coordinated, international set of economic arrangements. They did well. Their contributions significantly forges systems of cooperation between governments which, in turn, encouraged global economic growth and development.

But, is it time now to revisit Bretton Woods, that location in the hills of New Hampshire, where half a century ago U.S. Treasury Secretary Harry Dexter White, British economist Lord Keynes, and many others, set the plans for the post-war multilateral economic system?

The question is not academic. It was being asked recently in an unprecedented scale in the annual meeting of the IMF and World Bank in Washington D.C. The questioning came for three critical reasons:

First, there is a widespread view that a strong supranational institution is urgently required in the currency arena. The IMF has been absorbed with medium-term economics assistance programmes and appears to be attaching low priority to its original purpose: the IMF's Articles of Agreement declare the Fund's purpose is: "To promote international monetary cooperation through a permanent institution which provides the machinery for consultation and collaboration on international monetary problems".

Second, the WTO has brought tempers to the boil in many developing countries and created fears. The WTOs failure is serving now as a stimulus for the growth of regional trade blocs, based upon major industrial countries and open to relatively few developing countries.

Third, the World Bank has taken a backseat when it has come to advancing Western support for the poorest nations. There was a time when the President of the World Bank would use his office to rally international opinion and publicly urge the industrial nations to take a more constructive and more generous approach to the developing nations. In recent times the leadership of the institution has been silent. It has become mired in administrative matters, willing to bow to IMF leadership and content to seek to influence development thinking through the publication of economic research reports.

World Bank Subordinate to IMF

At the same time, the World Bank has come to play second fiddle to the IMF. The Fund has engineered itself into a position of leadership in economic policy discussion with developing countries and with the former command economies of East Europe and Central Asia. The World Bank does not provide programme lending of any kind until a borrowing country first has an IMF programme in place. While the two institutions are totally distinct in legal and financial terms, the Bank has accepted a subordinate position to the IMF.

These three phenomena are not encouraging for the health of global economy and from the perspective, in particular, of the developing countries.

On the monetary front there is a need to protect the interests of developing and emerging countries from the vagaries of the super-economic powers. Most of the governments of the world have looked on hopelessly as Japan, Germany and the United States, have pursued nationalist economic policies that have played havoc with the currency system. Most of the world's trade is booked in the currencies of these three countries and when those currencies spin out of control, so concluding trade deals and securing investment agreements becomes far more complex.

Uncertainty and instability in the world's currency systems are menaces that the IMF was expressly designed to counter. But the IMF has become so engaged in development lending (it now talks of providing programmes to some 80 countries) that its need for financial resources of its own is growing rapidly. That need makes it difficult for the Fund to be critical of its most powerful members. It cannot bite the hands that feed it. Thus, calls to the major nations for fiscal restraint, monetary discipline and international cooperation are made in muted tones.

The Fund, however, must respond to the mounting recognition that some supranational mechanisms are needed to survey the international economic landscape, to ring the alarm bells, to push and shove for meaningful consultation and to place blame on those whose policies are so nationalistic that they endanger the international system. IMF surveillance of the major economic power needs teeth.

The Fund should concentrate once again on using its influence and its expert staff to enhance international understanding of the complexities of the global trading and financial system. By this means it can rebuild its influence with the major powers. While it is unrealistic at this juncture to call for the IMF to become the world's central bank, it could serve as a vitally important convener of consultative processes designed to attain the objectives that its founders decreed: "To facilitate the expansion and balanced growth of international trade, and to contribute thereby to the promotion and maintenance of high levels of employment and real income and to the development of the productive resources of all members as primary objectives of economic policy".

The IMF's role should be enhanced. It should blend its monetary miles with new trade roles. The WTO been the forum for negotiations and for the supervisions of agreements. WTO does not undertake projects, it does not have powers to influence the policies of its most powerful members and it does not have the prestige needed to provide real leadership. It is time that the WTO was merged into the IMF.

Trade and Finance Belong Together

It makes little sense to split issues of international capital flows from trade questions. The globalisation of trade and investment has brought these disciplines close together. If forging satisfactory agreements is often difficult, then this in part is due to the fact that distinct organisations have leadership for distinct parts (WTO for trade and IMF for money) and there is no effective mechanism for cooperation. It is also the case that within national governments the trade and finance ministries are often in conflict and face insufficient pressure to coordinate. If the IMF managed both trade and monetary negotiations on the global scale, then this would add pressures on trade and finance ministers to work together.

Returning to its original monetary roles and adding a major trade role should be more than enough to keep the IMF busy. It would be logical, particularly in such circumstances, that the Fund return to the World Bank the development financing roles that it has assumed in recent years and that diverted it from its original purposes.

The IMF's Articles stress that one of its purposes is "to give confidence to members by making the general resources of the Fund temporarily available to them under adequate safeguards, thus providing them with opportunity to correct maladjustment in their balance of payments without resorting to measures destructive of national or international prosperity"

The Fund might argue that the World Bank should confine itself to infrastructure and social project finance and technical assistance and leave all programmes lending to the IMF. The reality is that the World Bank discovered to an increasing degree, starting with experiences with Turkey in 1979 and then with many highly indebted nations from 1982 onwards, that the best development projects will fail in countries where wholly unsatisfactory economic policies are in place. The Bank has also recognised the pain and complexity of adjustment and that countries embarking on adjustment policies enter upon a multi-year process: a process better geared to types of financing arrangements that the World Bank can offer, than those provided by the IMF.

Avoid Duplication of Effort Between IMF and World Bank

The experiences of the last decade have strengthened the World Bank's understanding of macro-economic policy reform and enhanced its capacity to provide comprehensive policy from support to its member countries. Cooperation with the IMF has improved, but it is also second best option and an expensive one. There remains too much duplication between the Fund and the Bank. The biggest cost is paid by the borrowing countries—ministers and their immediate subordinates spend endless hours negotiating separately with IMF and World Bank teams and developing duplicative reports.

Reform is only necessary when things are not working well. Today there is enormous scope for improvement in the global trading, monetary and development areas. The three prime institutions created for these areas are not performing well enough. Reform is urgent: the WTO should be merged with the IMF, the IMF should refocus on issues fundamental to securing a healthy global monetary (and trading) system and withdraw from the aid game: and the World Bank should have enlarged scope and provide more leadership on the development front.

Such reforms will not end the problems that our world economic system faces and their significance will be largely determined by the support they receive from the leaders of the most powerful industrial nations, irrespective of the zeal of the officials within the IMF and World Bank. Today, in the midst of prolonged international slump where nobody is satisfied with the ways in which the international system is operating, there is an important opportunity to secure backing in the capitals of the world's super-economic power for the types of reform that are articulated here.

10

Caught in the Debt Trap?

The Foreign Indebtedness of Developing Countries

The question of whether there is a way out of the developing countries' debt trap can only be properly answered if their indebtedness is not viewed as an isolated factor. It should be seen in the context of the total net resource flows into these countries. The following facts must be borne in mind:

1. Net resource flows to developing countries increased from 1994 to 1995 by 11.5 per cent of US $ 231.3 bn. The greatest share was made up of private sector flows, which accounted for 72 per cent ($ 167.1bn) of total transfer inputs.

2. Of the private flows, foreign direct investments totaling $ 90.3 bn dominate. Their well above average increase reflects the globalisation of production and growing integration of developing and transformation countries in the world economy. To date, however, this has applied mainly to 12 countries on which about 80 per cent of private inflows is concentrated. These are China, Mexico, Brazil, South Korea, Malaysia, Argentina, Indonesia, Thailand, Russia, India, Turkey and Hungary.

3. Portfolio equity flows to developing countries known for their high sensitivity on earnings and policy have dropped markedly for the time being to $ 22 bn. This is a not unexpected reaction to:

- the sharp rise in US interest rates since February 1994 and a very positive trend on the American capital market;
- the Mexican Peso crisis which began in December 1994; and
- the more cautious evaluation of the risks of investments in emerging markets, which major institutional investors believe have reached a certain degree of saturation.

4. Official development finance totalled $ 64.2 bn. of which, the World Bank reported, $ 11 bn was allocated to the rescue action for Mexico alone. ODA in 1995 stagnated at $ 47 bn. Its proportion of the OECD donor countries' GDPs was 0.29 per cent, the lowest since the beginning of the 1970s. The main reasons for this downturn where the industrial nations' well-known public budget problems and the fact that more creditworthy development and transformation countries are increasingly procuring their finance on private capital markets. Understandably, large sums were made available, mainly by Germany, to Eastern Europe and the successor states to the former Soviet Union. From strictly developmental viewpoints, it is disquieting that ever fewer ODA funds are available for longer-term development projects due to their disbursement for short-term emergency and crisis assistance.

The Washington Decisions

The recent annual conference of G7 finance ministers and central bank chiefs took the following decisions:

1. About 20 highly indebted poor countries (HIPCs) were to be reviewed to establish whether in endeavouring to solve their debt problems they could expect greater support from the international donor community than previously. There was a justified fear that without enhanced assistance, and continuing to employ only the

instruments used to date, these countries would not even achieve an acceptable level of indebtedness within the next 5-10 years.

2. Time horizon: in two three-year stages, a comprehensive review of the indebtedness and adjustment measures the affected countries could cope which would be undertaken. This would include observing the impacts of employing the customary instruments of debt relief. If the results were unsatisfactory, the new measures decided in Washington, which were expected to achieve a positive breakthrough, would be applied as well after three to six years. In detail, these are:

   - Paris Club (official creditors): rescheduling of bilateral debts, with case-to-case remission of up to 80 per cent compared with a current ceiling of 67 per cent;
   - comparable relief conditions through non-Paris Club and private creditors (London Club);
   - IMF: grants from the Enhanced Structural Adjustment Facility (ESAF) or long-term ESAF loans. The recipient countries use these sums for debt servicing; and
   - redemption of multilateral debts from a future HIPC trust fund to be administered by the IDA. Setting up the fund will formally ensure that it is not a matter of debt remission.

3. Financing: provisional estimates put the cost of the HIPC initiative at around $ 6 bn. This is to be funded by the Paris Club members, third-party creditors and international finance institutions. Two factors of the total costs are uncertain.

These are the number of countries which in the end will be given access to the funds, and the realism of the estimates of export income upon which the country analyses are based.

4. Assessment: all in all, the HIPC initiative is a fresh attempt to substantially relieve these countries of their debt problems, and support their economic reform programmes and measures to alleviate poverty. The World Bank and IMF were directed to begin implementing the debt initiative without delay and report back to the conference of the supervisory bodies in the spring of this year. Leading donor countries were able to agree to the initiative because:

   - financial integrity, particularly the preferential creditor status of the World Bank, the IMF and the regional development banks, was not in question;
   - The debtor countries were not relieved of their basic responsibility for comprehensive and sustainable adjustment policies; and finally;
   - The usual case-to-case procedure, taking decisions from country to country, was retained.

Global Impacts

To complete the "indebtedness picture", two other important problem areas must be pointed out. The problems and risks arising from the HIPCs' indebtedness affect first and foremost the national and, at worst, the regional level of the countries concerned. A serious endangering of the global finance and currency system must not be allowed to emanate from them. However, and this is the first problem, it can be much graver in the case of advanced developing countries, as Mexico showed in 1995. The risks which arise for the money and capital markets from liberalisation of short-term movements of capital in a number of threshold countries with large issue volumes are considerable. Strictly speaking, the capital market securities acquired in these markets by nationals and foreigners are only partly foreign debts. However, because they can be sold at any time and their convertibility and transferability is guaranteed, they can present similarly high risks for the solvency of the country concerned as "traditional" foreign debts. Additionally, the fact that "maturity" here depends not on contractually agreed terms, but on fragile investor confidence, enhances, the risks.

The large sums deployed in the Mexico rescue action organised by the USA and IMF show that endangerment of the international finance system was on hand. Above all, what the financial world aptly labelled the "Tequila effect" – a chain reaction of investors making a mass flight out of other threshold countries such as Brazil, Argentina and the Philippines, which threatened to spread—called for comprehensive confidence-building measures.

Not least, this experience was the basis for the agreement by the G7 ministers and central bankers in Washington on initial steps of a new IMF crisis financing mechanisms. Thus, the General Agreement on Credits was doubled to Special Drawing Rights of $ 34 bn.

Conclusion

The conclusions that must be drawn from this development are:

- to strengthen the IMF's role as a catalyst and improve its surveillance function;
- to bring the G7 group in their own interest to put in place stable economic general conditions, above all harmonised control of the interest rates of the key currencies; and
- to support the threshold countries in creating credible political conditions, especially by stabilising their economic, financial and currency policies in order to give no cause for sudden crises of confidence.

11

Rural Poverty in India

"It is morning in a remote farming area in India. As her husband harnesses a bullock to plough their field, a women pounds the grain she will use for the day's main meal. Three kilometres away, their children are collecting fuel wood and water before starting their morning walk to school".

"After School, they help their mother light a fire with a few sticks, milk the cow and collect the sundried grain. That evening, as the family rests around the hearth, father worries about how to sell his onions before they spoil and the price falls. Before sleeping his wife prepares a basket of home-grown vegetables to sell next day at the village market five kilometres away. With the takings, she hopes to buy a kerosene lamp although she might not have enough cash left to buy the kerosene immediately.."

That description of rural life is a daily reality for hundreds of millions of families throughout India. Rural poverty, 1990s means subsistence on the meagre earnings of wage labour or unreliable harvests from small plots of land. It means raising a family without safe drinking water or proper sanitation, suffering disease or injury without medical assistance. In times of unemployment or crop failure, it means living with the pangs of hunger—and the risk of death by famine.

Inside the Poverty Trap

Poverty in rural India is created and perpetuated by a number of closely interlined socio-economic processes.

1. Policies and institutional arrangements biased against the poor exclude them from the benefits of development, frustrate their productive potential and accentuate the impact of other poverty processes.

Institutional processes that perpetuate rural poverty include lack of access to land, inequitable share-cropping and tenancy arrangements, poor markets, limited access to credit, inputs and technology, and ineffective extension services. Other constraints are lack of training facilities, inadequate research related to smallholder farming system, and last but not least a lack of grassroots institutions needed to foster people's participation.

Policy and institutional biases have short and long-term impacts. In the short term, the poor are unable to earn enough to meet nutritional requirements or to take advantage of the market. "In the longer term", "poor households continue to lag behind because they do not generate a surplus for investment, nor do they have access to investment opportunities. Moreover, the rural poor may be forced to overuse resources, which undermines productivity and income".

2. Even today dualistic agrarian structures originating in colonial times persist. In Indian, highly capitalised large and medium-sized farms have virtually monopolistic control over land and labour at the expense of the small farm sector. Large scale commercial producers—control the best farm land. Resources have been funnelled into irrigated plantations producing cotton and mechanised cultivation of sorghum. In marginal areas, mechanisation has led to environmental degradation and the loss of seasonal grazing and stock routes for pastoralists.

"Thus, side by side with modern agriculture, millions of marginal farmers and herdsmen subsist far below the poverty line". This dualism severely limits their capacity to grow food and accumulate capital. They lack marketable surpluses, and incentives and opportunities to save and invest.

3. Rapid population growth can cause and perpetuate rural poverty by increasing pressure on limited productive resources, social services and employment, as well as paradoxically—creating labour shortage through outmigration.

The most obvious consequence of rapid population growth is that, even with relatively high rates of economic growth, improvements in living conditions are limited. Total saving in the economy declines, leaving fewer resources for investment in human development. Negative consequence are most acute in rural areas. Growing population often combined with traditional laws of inheritance—has led to fragmentation of holdings, degradation of crop and pasture land, and falling yields. In areas with unequal distribution of land, rapid population growth has accelerated proletarisation of the rural work force and reduced incomes.

4. Rural poverty malnutrition and undernutrition are closely linked to environmental degradation. Poor people in marginal areas are destroying natural resources as they struggle to keep their production systems sustainable. In acute shortage of arable land has forced farmers to reduce the length of fallow periods and plough up land previously reserved for grazing. These practices have led to declining yields, soil depletion and further impoverishment. Population pressure is pushing weaker members of the rural community into ecologically vulnerable areas.

Degradation of the environment is strongly linked to household food insecurity and lack of fuel. Much of the fragile forest cover has been destroyed by poor rural people in the search for grazing land and fuel wood.

Government policies have also wrought environmental damage. A rapid expansion of areas under crops often accelerates deforestation and land degradation. Programmes to expand cereal production into marginal areas, subsidised capital to support commercial operations subsidies for inappropriate technologies and excessive transfer of income out of the agricultural sector may undermine the sustainability of smallholers and pastoralists' production systems.

Inadequate public investment in off-farm employment and infrastructure, a lack of price incentives and inadequate access to modern agricultural inputs and services discourage investment in land conservation, leading to further overuse and degradation.

5. As poverty undermines traditional social bond, the marginalisation of women has become a fact of rural life in India. With little or no access to land, million of women depend on casual employment on meagre wages. Often, they farm fragmented plots of poor quality. Limited access to inputs, extension, training and credit limits, in turn, their ability to enter commercial agriculture.

The exodus of males in search of work in urban areas (itself an indicator of poverty) has serious consequences for the women they have leave behind. Output from land often falls and less attention is paid to maintenance, setting the stage for a long-term decline in productivity. Many female headed households have abandoned the use of oxen for ploughing, some plough and plant late and others no longer weed their fields.

6. The ethnic or cultural marginalisation of tribal or minority populations also plays a role in poverty. Many of these groups are further threatened by newly marginalised groups—as the expansion of cultivation reduces and grazing areas of nomadic herders.

7. Exploitative middlemen also perpetuate rural poverty. Landlords exploit share croppers and tenants, moneylenders exploit debtors, and traders exploit small scale producers. During seasonal food shortages, the poor may have to borrow money at interest rates

exceeding 20 per cent a month. Forced to devote most of their energies to debt servicing, they sink deeper into the poverty trap.

In some cases, government controlled co-operatives and government agencies whose task is to protect the poor may themselves practise forms of exploitation. Heavy levies imposed by government agencies have damaged small farmers. Large, inefficient bureaucracies are paid for by the productive sectors of the community and frequently contribute to accumulation of large budget deficits.

8. Political troubles and civil strife have had a disastrous impact on the rural poor one effect is the disruption of development assistance to the rural poor, both from national and international agencies. Another is the transformation of many producers into consumers of social services with serious consequences for production, savings, capital accumulation and investment.

9. The international economic environment directly influences the well-being of the Indian poor. Falling commodity prices and projectionist policies in India affect the employment and incomes of plantation workers and smallholders producing for export, particularly those relying heaving on a few agricultural commodities. Change in international interest rates have repeatedly hurt smallscale producers in debt-burdened India, While world grain price increases has triggered rural famines.

The net flow of development resources to agriculture also affects rural poverty. Official development funding for food and agriculture increased between 1975 and 1982, but has fluctuated irregularly since. Moreover, concern with trade balances is diverting resources to export crops, sometimes at the expense of traditional crops grown by poor farmers.

12

The Dynamics of Rural Poverty in India

Poverty is homogeneous only when considered from the point of view of income or consumption: the uniformity of the poor as a category exists only on the level of the fact that they have little to consume. When considered from the point of view of production, i.e., the circumstances in which the poor must operate to gain their income, the conditions of poverty are extraordinary diverse. A concrete grasp of these diverse circumstances is the first step in developing relevant instruments to address not only the problems of the poor, but also the challenge of taking advantage of the opportunities available to them.

The conventional means of measuring economic progress, such as Gross National Product per cpita, tell us little about the real nature of poverty. In recent years this sort of yardstick has been supplemented by measurements of food security, income distribution, and social development (encompassing health and education). These offer the possibility of composite indices, allowing the development of more rounded characterisations and comparisons of poverty at the national level. However, these principally refer to the symptoms of poverty, not to the relational factors generating it. Poverty is not a state of being, it is the effect of dynamic processes. While it is important to know where poverty is greatest, it is critical to know why it exists. This inquiry necessarily leads away from the nature of the poor as individuals to the nature of their social and physical environment. Poverty is not only a personal phenomenon, it is a social status. As such, while its effects can be measured on the level of the individual, its causes must be sought elsewhere. From the point of view of poverty alleviation the process of becoming is just as important as the state of being.

At the heart of poverty is the inadequate access of the poor to productive resources. Low incomes tend to reflect inadequate means of production, not incompetent producers. However, poverty in India is not simply a reflection of private resources. A broad range of "external" factors impinge on incomes, among them the following:

National Policies

One of the ironies of Indian development is that while no government wants poverty, many policies contribute to it—what is given in anti-poverty programme is drained away by other policies. The poor do not always come out ahead in the balance—they are often net "donors" to the rest of society. Frequent reference is made to unsustainable forms of development—to urban over-expansion, industrialisation based on subsidies, and to public sector engorgement. What is less frequently realised is that the bill for these phenomena is often presented to the rural poor. Taxation of exports to sustain sectors with little export potential of their own and subsidised food imports to supply the urban population are policies that are often paid for by the rural poor. In many areas of India, exports are agricultural goods produced by small farmers. Here export taxes contribute to rural poverty. The same is true of "cheap" food imports which depress the prices paid to small farmers for their food crops.

"Structural imbalance" is not only a recipe for increasing external indebtedness, it is also a recipe for increasing the poverty of the rural population. The political weakness of the poor in most areas is not only the basis for inadequate poverty alleviation programmes and policies—it is the basis for an actual transfer of their income to more socially influential groups. While it is often correctly asserted that the poor are the first to suffer from adjustments involving public social expenditure cuts it is often the case that they also have the most to gain from the elimination of policy-based economic distortions that reflect social power rather than productive efficiency and potential.

Demographic Factors

Accelerated population growth is a long-term contributor to poverty. In India the incomes of the poor have declined, mortality rates are also falling, pushing the numbers up. In the meantime, land is becoming scarcer, plots more fragmented and the soil and pasture increasingly degraded. This phenomenon is not without its policy dimensions. As long as the poor remain undercapitalised, and essential determinant of household income is the amount of labour available to it household economic strategies favour large families. While population policy has a role to play, possibly more critical is a change in the economic environment. Access to capital and more secure income changes perceptions of the need for labour. In the medium and long-term, population dynamics are driven by the underlying productive systems. As long as the production systems of the poor remain underdeveloped, population growth remains high, restricting even the future possibility of development.

Natural Resource Management and the Environment

If poverty is both cause and effect of rapid population expansion, so poverty is both cause and effect of many dimensions of degradation of the environment. Many of the rural poor, but by no means all, live in areas of extreme environmental fragility, a circumstance often prompted by high level of control by the better-off over more stable and productive resource areas. Here the poor are extraordinarily exposed to the dangers of erosion, whittling away at an already meager productive base. The threat is not entirely due to nature. Rather, poverty accelerates erosion. Without capital, the poor are frequently unable to invest in even traditional methods of soil and water conservation. And without sufficient land they are forced to shorten fallow periods, putting further strain on the resource base. As in the case of population growth, the result is strain not only on the poor, but on the entire Indian economy. Given the extremely limited economic alternatives, the solution to this problem is not to forbid the use of environmentally fragile resources to the poor, it is to change the conditions under which their use takes place. Access to conservation technology is important; but more so are security of land tenure and resources to invest.

Combating poverty means not only increasing the production of the poor, but also preserving and enhancing the long-term value of the resource they control. What this very often means, in practice is assisting the poor in reestablishing a stable relationship with fragile resource. Prevailing processes in many areas invovle the gradual—and sometimes not so gradual—depletion of natural resources, to the detriment of all. Part of the answer to this is conservation. Part of the answer is also to provide viable economic alternatives to the poor, reducing their dependence on erosion-prone crop and livestock practices.

Exploitative Intermediates

The poor are not unaware of the pressure upon them, and also of means of overcoming them. Their ability to respond, however, is severely impaired by social powerlessness. The poor are surrounded by a dense network of public and private factors reducing their freedom of action, and actually draining what few resources they do have. Members of the network include traders and moneylenders capitalising upon the economic weakness of the poor, and engaging them in unequal exchanges. They also include public agencies either indifferent to the requirements of the socially uninfluential, or actively engaged in extracting "surplus" for use by other groups. Not to be excluded from this are organisations which are ostensibly "for" the poor, but which, in fact, serve as systems of containment and control.

13

Rural Poverty in India and Development as a Policy Challenge

Poverty can be overcome, and that the poor can increase their income and production within an appropriate framework. Part of that framework is made up of a flow of resources and local-level institutional development, and there is considerable scope for improvement in both. However, the impact of investment and organisation is strictly determined by the nature of the policy environment. While project and programmes can bring some relief to the rural poor, substantial change needs a strong policy commitment. While the poor can overcome poverty, they will not be able to until this becomes a major focus of national policy and action. In the main, this sort of commitment has not been made in the past—at the expense of both the poor and overall development in many areas.

The current state of India is highly contradictory. On the one hand, there is proclamation of a new order; on the other, increasing value is given to sectional and short-term national and group interests. With an overt concern with the India's poor goes an equal weight given to concern with economic mechanisms and relations that pay little attention to poverty and foster more inequality. The dangers of this situation are real. The lack of concrete attention being given to change will mean greater economic polarisation. Greater polarisation among the better-off, and between the better-off and the poor—means instability and a lack of consensus, a lack of legitimacy.

Poverty is far-reaching, and ought to be curtailed. In a period in which resources everywhere appear restricted, this seems not to be an attractive proposition at the practical level. Welfare is everywhere giving way to production as an imperative, just as public expenditure is giving way to private accumulation. Poverty alleviation does not appear to be an idea whose time has come. The objections are great, but they are also misplaced. Poverty alleviation is not necessarily a drain upon accumulation, and it is not primarily a public activity. Poverty alleviation is primarily the activity of the poor themselves, and their progress necessarily involves productive expansion. If this potential for private expansion has not been realised, it is not because of the nature of the poor, it is because of the way in which national economic affairs have been organised. Economic policy has been oriented towards the better off—not infrequently at the expense of the poor. Given the historic association between wealth and power, the definition of development in terms of the large and the wealthy is hardly surprising.

There is the possibility of associated growth involving both large-scale and small-scale production, the better of and the poor. The realisation of this possibility might result from a new social compact. This social compact is not a commitment to social safety nets and welfare, both of which seem to presuppose that the poor are somehow necessarily out of the growth field. It is a commitment to abolishing artificial and onerous terms of exchange that discriminate against the poor, to investing resources where there are real opportunities for gain, irrespective of whether the economic agents concerned are rich or poor, and to creating the space for the poor to organise to pursue their social and economic interests.

There is a need for a new growth model consistent with new social realities. While the 1980s was a period of clearing away many of the obstacles to development, it was not a period in which there emerged a clear vision of what represented the positive basis for growth, beyond, that is, a general prescription of market-driven operations. The model must pass from admonition to positive prescription to fuel growth by integrating the poor in their rightful place in the production function. It must redefine the position of public expenditure in the development process, and seek to establish market structures which are both equitable and open to the participation of the economically weaker elements of the population. Most of all it must revalue the position and contribution of the poor and small-scale producers in the growth process, particularly in the agricultural sector, but not exclusively agriculture.

This means that the issue is not so much one of less government, but of government, both national and local, finding a new rationale for action, including, *inter alia*, creating conditions that will effectively unleash the productive potential of the rural poor.

Financial flows to the poorest Indians are not likely to undergo a very major expansion, especially through private channels. Development will rely very much on the mobilisation of their own resources, and many of these resources are in the hands of the poor, are, indeed, not only the human capital embodied in the poor but also their assets which, while small, individually are cumulatively important in India. The growth model for the 1990s will have to embrace that fact, and build upon it. The paradox of most development models is that they have emphasised the value of what Indians do not have, while devaluing what they have: capital intensity has been promoted in situations of scarcity of capital, at the expense of abundant labour and of low-cost methods of manifold increase of the productivity of assets of which the poor do dispose. In a not very indiret way, the creation of poverty has been subsidised. Poverty alleviation is neither a special topic nor a low-cost substitute for growth. Is is neither more nor less "social" than development in general. It is part of the formulation of any sustainable strategy of economic development. In the 1990s it may, and perhaps should, become the dominant issue—not as an alternative to the structural reorganisations of the 1980s, but as a means of filling a growth framework with substance.

14

The Persistence of Indian Poverty and Its Alleviation

Poverty has always been with us and for at least forty years its alleviation has been the professed objective of many strategies to improve the lot of the Indians. But the way in which it has been conceived, however, has been subject to considerable change. Relatively little attention was paid to the development of the poor themselves. Rather, they were portrayed as among the beneficiaries of development in larger systems which were to provide the dynamic force for the elimination of poverty (from the "outside," as it were). Development was principally something that happened to the poor—on a "trickle-down" basis.

The simple assumption that the poor would benefit from general economic growth, without paying any special attention to them, changed somewhat in the late 1950s, when it was perceived that the poor might not automatically benefit from macro-economic development, but that they must benefit if the social stability needed for overall economic growth was to be assured. From this point there emerged a specific line of antipoverty thinking to improve the income of poor people.

The manner in which the poor were to be integrated into the overall growth process, however, was very specific. It was concerned not so much with what the poor could offer to the growth process—as with what they should receive from that process. For all its merits the Basic Needs strategy, and the social "safety net" approach which followed it, basically emphasised the consumption needs of the poor—and not their surplus producing possibilities. On the contrary, a persistent theme in the discourse about the economics of the poor has been the need for some sort of transfer of resources to them from more productive and dynamic sectors of accumulation. In short, the poor have been portrayed as a net burden on the growth process.

It is possible to introduce an element of differentiation into this picture: given that it is rarely alleged that low wages are an obstacle to accumulation and growth, the poor who have been characterised as a burden have tended to be those not directly integrated into nascent large-scale systems of production: these are the poor "peripheral" to modern economic process—a group which encompasses a large proportion of the urban population in India (principally employed in the "informal" sector), as well as a vast mass of small, but relatively independent agricultural producers.

Implicitly, then, the concepts of "peripheral", small-scale and poor have been run together to form, in the realm of ideas, a more or less dependent mass. The number of people ostensibly in these categories is huge, and they seem to represent an enormous burden on development. They represent a development "problem", and an awesome one at that.

While substantial progress has been made in India in reducing the percentage of the rural population below nationally defined poverty line, the absolute number of the rural poor has increased. The growth of output did not bring about a significant improvement in the income share of the lowest nor a uniform reduction in the percentage of the rural population below the poverty line. The situation actually worsened. Less than half of the rural population in India has access to safe water or sanitation, and only 60 per cent had any access to health services. National data on life expectancy, infant mortality and literacy show improvements, but also the persistence of completely unacceptable conditions.

The pursuit of growth has not solved the development problem. Trickle-down has not worked or it has not worked enough. The massive persistence of poverty, particularly in rural areas represents a problem for the popular acceptance of continued economic adjustment; and it represents a problem for growth itself. The problem lies not only in the unintended consequences of the prevailing development paradigm, but in the viability of the paradigm itself. Part of the debt crisis arose from an inability to mobilise fully domestic assets, and from systematic resort to external resources. The unsustainability of this form of development has been amply demonstrated. Part of the answer to the challenge of development lies in a greater and more appropriate use of the resources of developing countries themselves.

A substantial part of these assets can be created by the poor who have been so marginal to past development efforts. The poverty of a nation and the poverty of people are not as easily separable as was often thought in the past. In many cases, it is difficult to envisage national growth without strong economic development among the poor themselves—not us objects, but as subjects of development. The fact that this is insufficiently perceived is as much an expression of the development of social and economic interests as it is of the development or otherwise of economic theory. Development has frequently been associated with large-scale production and large-scale inputs of capital, and these new social and economic patterns have often defined development in their own image, i.e., in terms of the centrality of large-scale production and accumulation.

Poverty Alleviation

The perspective is not that growth achieved by the better-off will pull the poor out of poverty, but that the mobilisation and enhancement of the resources and activities of the poor themselves can uphold their dignity and free them from the shackles of misery, while at the same time making a vital contribution to overall sustainable growth.

Individually and collectively, the obstacles facing the poor are formidable. They are, however, not insuperable. Most of the forces creating poverty are essentially social. They reflect systems of resources allocation that are made by societies, and as such they can be reversed. Pricing policies, credit systems, and social and productive services, which neglect the poor, as well as gender discrimination, are not natural, universal and inevitable facts—and neither is the poverty they give rise to. One of the major obstacles to overcome in fighting poverty is the perception of poverty itself—and of the poor. In this regard, perhaps the most important point is that the poor are not idle, they work. Nobody is simply "poor". In other words, it is not just a state of being. In this regard, "poor" is more aptly used as an adjective rather than as a noun. The rural poor are poor farmers, poor herders and poor fishermen. In short, they are poor producers: their incomes are gained from their work. The answer to poverty lies in creating the conditions for them to earn more from their work. From this perspective, overcoming poverty does not mean less growth, it is a contributor to growth—for it means making the poor more productive. Too often in the past poverty alleviation has been seen as a burden on the economy, as involving a transfer of something for nothing in exchange. It need not be that way: it can be an investment in production, benefiting both poor and the national economy. Poverty has been defined as a production problem, and poverty alleviation as an investment.

Nobody wishes to be poor, and few accept it passively. The poor are rarely without initiative. What they lack are the means of pursuing it. In no small measure, overcoming poverty involves building upon this initiative and will, helping organise cooperation, and providing material support. This support does not have to take the form of handouts. The problem of the poor is not that they cannot handle resources efficiently, but they do not have access to them.

The challenge of creating an institutional framework for credit for the poor is an expression of the general institutional challenge facing poverty alleviation: institutions are not oriented to the poor. Many factors enter into this, ranging from the costs of working with a large number of unorganised people, to the prevalence of myths about the improvidence of the poor, to a simple desire on the part of the better-off to monopolize scarce resources. The answer to this is to create institutional responsiveness, either through introducing demand-led organisation into existing institutions concerned with the poor or through promoting institutions created by the poor themselves. In both cases, participation by the poor is critical. The objective is not only to mobilize the individual initiatives of the poor, but also to mobilize their collective strength and capabilities. As individuals, many of the poor are virtually unreachable. As members of associations and groups they create their own channels for institutional access.

The poor as producers; the poor as credit-worthy handlers of material assistance; the poor as institutional actors—these are not elements of theory, but of practice and experience. Notwithstanding the growing acceptance of the need to do something "about" the poor, not everyone shares this understanding of poverty. As long as the poor are viewed from afar, the myths of poverty and the poor persist. Even those who over reemphasise the need for social "safety nets" and handouts, while ostensibly helping the poor, maintain the image of helplessness, and of the need to do something "for" them. A closer view reveal something very different: tremendous work and initiative on the part of the poor, both based on their desire to do something for themselves. This is not a burden, it is an extraordinary social and economic asset. Again, viewed from a distance, poverty looks overwhelming. The closer view reveals very specific situations of opportunities and needs. These can be responded to—not only through soup kitchens, which should be seen as desirable in addressing emergencies only—but through strengthening the individual and collective means available to the poor to carve out their own path of independence and growth. The dynamics of poverty are reversible, but only in collaboration with the poor themselves.

Precisely because of past neglect of the poor as producers, a neglect involving a failure to involve them in the process of technological development, organisation, and capitalisation, the gap between the current and potential production of the poor is enormous. Investment in the poor is not a loss-making enterprise. Poverty is less a failure of the poor, than a failure of policy-makers to grasp their potential. Far from there being a tradeoff between poverty and growth, the persistence of poverty represents a limit to growth.

Mobilising and enhancing the ability of the rural poor to expand their own income and contribute to national growth is not simply a process of raising incomes. It involves structural change in economies and societies. It involves helping the poor to position themselves securely within main-line economic processes. This means first increasing and improving their access to land—by land reform, land-titling, better management and better conservation, supported, where necessary, by irrigation, new technologies and improved infrastructure. Secondly, it means increasing the productivity and use of rural labour, emphasizing labour intensive technology and better training for new skills. Thirdly, it means making more capital available to the rural poor, mobilizing savings, providing infrastructure and developing financial services tailored to their situation and needs.

Not least, it mean acknowledging the important contribution of poor women in all of these areas of activity. At present, the contribution of women to the rural economy is seriously underestimated—the "invisible women" syndrome. Official statistics rarely make any effort to measure it, even though it is more than clear that not just unpaid household work but the farm and trading activities of women make a vital and significant contribution to the well-being of poor rural households. All the evidence suggests that the poorer the household the more hour's women work and the greater their investment in both economic production and family welfare. From a situation of multiple disadvantage as poor, as women and often as single parents, women can move to one in which they contribute and benefit three-fold—in the home, in society at large and, not least, in the development of the next generation.

Many of the measure that need to be taken to allow the poor to realize their potential do not involve more expenditures; they involve the elimination of economic distortions against the rural poor. These distortions have effectively taxed the poor, and mainly the rural poor, in favour of inappropriate and inefficient urban developments whose support has been at the root of widespread economic crises. To no small extent, helping the poor make their potential contribution to development involves no more than creating a "level playing field" and, when conceived in such a light, structural adjustment can make a vital contribution to both resumed growth and social equity. It is often felt that the poor are somehow "outside" the scope of national economic policies. This is virtually never the case. They are affected by national economic policies, but this inclusion takes a very special form: exposure to the costs, and exclusion from the benefits. In this regard, there is a certain irony in the view that small-scale producers "need" subsidies to survive. In fact, it has been the development of large-scale production in agriculture (and industry) in India that has been heavily dependent upon subsidisation over the decades—benefits, which small-scale producers have rarely enjoyed.

This is characteristic of many forms of large-scale production in India—although nominally at the cutting edge of efficiency and productivity; it is they rather than the small-scale producers who have been dependent upon transfers and protection for their reproduction.

Change in the environment of poverty necessitates greater awareness of the root causes of poverty on the part of policy-makers. However, the realisation of the social and economic potential of the rural poor is not just a question of economic policy and investment. It also involves the development of a general social framework in which the economic and social interests of the poor can be freely articulated and responded to. It means instilling democratic and participatory values at every level in society and not just at the level of nationwide institutions. The most valid spokesmen of the poor are the poor themselves.

The opening of economic and social opportunities to the poor offers the possibility of more stable and sustainable change. The alternative is for societies to polarize further, for the welfare burden to grow to greater proportions and for a widening gap to develop between the modern and traditional sectors. In the end, the continued poverty of the rural areas will be a brake on the output of the advanced sector, eroding the potential for self-sustaining growth.

15

Overcoming the Poverty in India and the Lessons Learned

Basic elements in the struggle against poverty in India are the provision of the economic services and assets which the poor have tended not to receive in the past—as a result of oversight or design. The emphasis on economic services and assets is just because the mass of the rural poor are self-employed, and it is upon the improvement in the means of production directly accessible to them that their prosperity depends. Health and education are very important, but offer more if combined with the material means of making a living—of putting body and mind to work. These assets and services include land, water, technology, commercial services, handling output and inputs, and credit—provided within an economic policy famework conductive to their optimal exploitation.

This list is hardly new. It corresponds to the requirements of any producer. The basic points to be made in this regard are: firstly, that the general requirements of poor producers are precisely the same as those of other producers and that measures to alleviate poverty that fall short of recognising the full range of such requirements are doomed to failure; and, secondly, that these assets and services are not typically provided in a form accessible to the poor. India has made important progress in providing a more effective framework for agricultural production "in general", this framework has not properly embraced small and poor producers. They are as follows:

Access to Land and Water

In the case of access to land, for example, land reform efforts in India has frequently involved major loopholes, allowing the socially powerful to minimise *de facto* improvements in the condition of the poor. In the critical area of land rights, registration processes have been so complex and costly relative to the resources of the poor that land regularisation programmes have, sometimes unintentionally, become virtual characters for legalising the eviction of the poor and the actual loss of their traditional rights. Irrigation without specific measures to defend the interests of existing occupants of areas exposes them to expulsion—and, moreover, has tended to be concentrated in large-scale schemes benefiting already high potential areas in which the better-off predominate. While huge sums have been spent on large-scale irrigation schemes, little has been spent on water conservation and the sort of small-scale developments that are more likely to be of relevance to marginal small-scale producers.

Technology Transfer

In the area of technology, attention has been focused on technologies (such as the Green Revolution) requiring extensive access to water and fertilisers, neither of which are generally available among the poor. In fact, research almost every where has concentrated on larger-scale production in areas of relatively high resource endowment. In contrast to this, research relevant to small-scale producers in marginal soil and rainfed areas in India has been shockingly deficient. As in other fields, this is partly explicable in terms of a frequently unproved belief that large-scale production is more efficient. It is also explicable in terms of the fact that it is the powerful who set the research agenda, not the poor. Taking its inspiration from highly specialised, large-scale agricultural units of production, research has tended to dwell separately on individual crops—rather than on the interaction between crops, which is of much greater relevance to small-scale producers engaging in highly complex systems of production to maximise food self-sufficiency and minimise risks.

Commercial Services

In the area of handling of output and inputs, organised services (not infrequently under public control in the past) have tended to concentrate in the proximity of large-scale producers and users of input in relatively well-endowed areas. In India the poor have had to incur the extraordinary costs of handling their own transport of goods to and from service points—frequently over long and deficient lines of communication. The alternative has been to resort to private intermediaries offering goods, and buying products, at prices very different from those enjoyed by larger producers. In effect, the better-off and the poor have confronted different sets of prices—with the poor paying more for what they buy, and receiving less for what they sell.

Credit

In the area of credit, the situation has been disastrous. It is generally recognised that productive improvement needs a change in means of production—new tools, improved seeds, fertilisers, etc. Such a change everywhere is typically effected on the basis of credit. Yet rural credit schemes in India have usually not extended support to small farmers and the poor. Credit has been concentrated among richer farmers with collateral and with demand for larger loans. In order to improve their productivity, the poor have been forced to seek credit from informal money-lenders—at virtually confiscatory rates. Again, the cost of modernisation has been much higher for the poor than for the better-off. The inevitable result has been a lower rate of change—and the consolidation, rather than the reduction of poverty.

The Victims Blamed

Although vast amounts of money have been invested in rural development in India, very little of it has reached the poor. The poor have been left to their own devices, while the better-off have received a wide range of assistance—not infrequently allowing them to encroach further upon the land of the poor. Support for agricultural expansion has not led to rural development, and it has not eliminated rural poverty. The relatively undynamic performance of many small-scale farmers under these circumstances is frequently taken as "proof" that they are a poor investment. This is a variant of "blaming the victim". In fact, the poor have fared badly, not because they could not efficiently use support, but because they did not get it.

In other words, the failure of the poor to benefit from agricultural sector investments has not reflected an economic failure among the poor themselves. Rather, it has involved policy and institutional failures. On the policy level, it has tended to reflect an unwillingness to restrain the socially influential from seeking to monopolise scarce resources to their own benefit—and, perhaps, a lack of awareness of the incompatibility between apparently "neutral" criteria for support (e.g., the demand for land title as collateral for credit) and the particular circumstances of poor and small farmers (e.g., involvement) in traditional forms of land tenure). On the institutional level, it has involved both unwillingness to give weight to the requirements of the poor, and a lack of initiative in solving real problems in providing services to the poor such as the high cost of providing services on an individual basis to a large number of small and often dispersed "clients". While there has been a great deal of lamentation about poverty in India, remarkably little has been done to change it at the level of economic systems—perhaps because social welfare activities are much easier to implement than real policy and institutional changes. It is possible to do very much better—not by simply pouring in more resources (in channels which at times do not even ultimately reach the poor), but by changing the framework of investment, i.e., the instruments of development.

LESSONS LEARNED

Targeting of Resources

The fundamental lessons learned are that investment resources must be targeted at the poor. In a world of competition for scarce resources, investments in rural development tend to be captured by those with national and local power—a group, which rarely encompasses the rural poor. The first step in delivering resources to the poor is establishing strict criteria for eligibility for assistance. Indicators of wealth in India vary according to the nature of the local economy—in some cases it is extent of land ownership, in others size of cattle herds, in yet others ownership of draught animals—but the principle remains the same: investment in those with the least assets. In some cases, for example, where women represent a significant proportion of actual producers, this may give rise to entirely new patterns of investment.

Reorienting Institutions

The intention to distribute resources to the poorest is not always accompanied by actual performance. Among the reasons for this is the inappropriateness of delivery mechanisms. Put simply, institutions long oriented to the non-poor have tended to develop operating procedures and structures which reflect the nature of their de facto clientele and which hinder them from serving a new target group. In the area of credit, for example, insistence upon collateral in land may be an absolute obstacle to participation by the poor—just as a limited banking network may represent an obstacle to delivery to the poor, for whom the costs of communicating with a bank at considerable distance might well add significantly to the real cost of credit. Effectively channeling resources to the poor, therefore, means the elaboration of institutional means of delivery consistent with their circumstances.

However, it must be recognised that there are exceptional institutional costs associated with providing services to (and among) the poor—costs arising from the fact that there are many individuals involved, and that their individual requirement tend to be quite small. The costs of government services in, for example, agricultural credit, are necessarily higher if this involves a very large number of small producers than if it involves a small number of large producers. Administration costs in banking tend to be much higher relative to loan volume if it involves a myriad of individual small loans. These factors have often been adduced as reasons for the "impossibility" of servicing the poor. Effective Service appears financially impossible, especially the context of widespread retrenchment in public expenditure under structural adjustment programmes. The poor are often willing to pay the actual costs of services—especially if the alternative is no service at all, or supply by local informal monopolists. On the other hand, there are proven ways of reducing costs of service supply to the poor—by involving the poor themselves. Everywhere in India poor people overcome some of the obstacles involved in their individual poverty through cooperation and joint action. While such organisation typically develops in the absence of formal service organisations and markets, it can also develop in association with formal organisations. In effect, the organised small farmer can help shoulder the cost of services through organizing local level distribution and administration themselves.

People's Participation

People's participation is, therefore, not only a "social" concept. It is an eminently economic concept, involving cost sharing. It is fundamental to the sustainability of improvements. The long-term solution is not to throw money at the problems of the poor, but to help them to organise to overcome then themselves. One of the happy externalities of this approach is not only lower cost services, but services more likely to be in harmony with what small farmers perceive themselves as needing.

Balanced Development

Development means change, not only in the volume of production, but in the composition of output and the conditions under which it is produced. What is argued is that the pursuit of development without the inclusion of the mass of small-scale producers and the poor has important structural drawbacks, and that their inclusion offers the basis for more sustainable long-term development. Some smallholder groups have a vast unutilised potential for expansion. Others have much more modest prospects.

Even those with the poorest assets and possibilities however, can be helped to improve their condition. While the direct economic benefits of this may be relatively slender, the side-effects may be great. An eventual shift of these groups to other areas and systems of production might be inevitable if aspirations for a better life are to be satisfied, but it is essential that this shift be orderly necessitating that support be given in the transitional period. This support can be either a direct welfare transfer or an investment in productive capacity. In many cases the latter may be the least-cost alternative.

The issue, then, is neither the "rich way" nor the "poor way". What is required is: an unprejudiced evaluation of the capacities and possibilities of poor and small-scale producers, and their potential role in the overall scheme of national development; allocation of investment resources according to potential and within an institutional framework ensuring delivery and profitable use; and a more balanced view of the overall social costs and benefits of alternative means of addressing transitional states. The belief is that the outcome of this will involve a reappraisal of the role of the poor in economic development, and a major improvement in the state of the rural poor throughout India.

The poor are many, their productive potential is great, but in few places is the exploitation of this potential an explicit focus of policy concern and action—although everywhere it is the concern of the poor themselves. While concrete evidence of the efficacy of systematic policy of support to the poor is sparse (simply because it has so rarely been tried), the evidence of its effectiveness on the local level is abundant.

16

Towards a New Policy on Poverty Reduction

In recent years, the call for the policy which enables the reduction of mass poverty in India has increased not only from scientific point of view, but also from political and practical standpoint. Mass poverty is a problem crucial not only for the people concerned, but also for the future of humanity as a whole, and one that cries out for rapid solution. Indians still have not succeeded in permanently improving the living conditions of big parts of their population. Measures in terms of economic growth expected by Indians over the past fifty years, the preliminary growth-oriented development strategies pursued hitherto have not been unsuccessful. Many poor population groups continue to be excluded from the economic growth. The "Trickle-down effect" has failed still fails to reach them.

Marginalisation

As a result, the course development took in India led to the marginalisation of broad sections of the population. Marginal groups arose that were denied access to the development process. They are characterised by a lack of active participation (exclusion from decision-making processes) and passive participation (failure to receive goods, services and social services). Such groups found themselves in a vicious circle. Because of their marginality they achieved only low rates of labour productivity and remained poor. They consequently slipped further towards the fringe of development. The greater the progress attained by the other sectors of the economy, the more acute the marginalisation process became. The numerical increase in membership of these marginal groups was so great that in course of time they came to constitute a considerable proportion of the population.

This mass poverty is unacceptable not only from a humanitarian point of view. It also engenders problems of global dimensions. The increasing threat to the environment, a population growth stretching the capacity of the earth to its very limits, dramatic difficulties in India safeguarding food supplies, and the still unresolved debt crisis are only the tip of an iceberg that is to a large extent spawned and nurtured by mass poverty.

In view of this situation it seems paradoxical that the scientific literature related to the problem of mass poverty apparently finds it difficult to precisely define poverty, to ascertain its causes and to asses it in ethical, political, social and economic terms. The literature often states that there is neither a generally acceptable definition nor a more or less comprehensive and stringent theory of poverty. However, the lack of generally binding definitions of the concept is due not to the often cited difficulty of measuring the societal "quality" of poverty in quantitative terms. The reason is rather that both societies as a whole and individual social groups with differing values, religious convictions, ideologies and the resulting structures and functions, reach differing conclusions on where the line between "poor" and "not poor" is to be drawn. Views differ just as widely on the societal and individual salience of poverty. A generally valid concept of poverty applicable to every social context is accordingly not available.

Absolute and Relative Poverty

In discussing the problems of poverty, a distinction must be drawn between absolute and relative poverty. In the case of absolute poverty the insufficiency of resources available to an economic entity for the maintenance of physical subsistence is so drastic that the affected parties are no longer able to live in a manner "fit for human being". In the case of relative poverty an economic entity has insufficient resources in comparison to other economic entities. This relative poverty does not necessarily mean that those affected are unable to live a life fit for human beings. It means merely that, due to the distributional structures prevailing in an economy, individual economic entities suffer deprivation to an unacceptable degree.

Poverty can be defined in both its aspects as deprivation. The deprivation can refer to various economic, social and/or political areas of human life. Poverty then means that various economic, social, and/or political needs of certain social groups are not satisfied, or are only inadequately satisfied. How drastic deprivation must be in individual cases and in what areas it has to occur before one can speak of absolute or relative poverty depends both on the observer's concept of tolerance and standards and on the given frame of reference.

The attempt to formulate an objective and generally valid definition of poverty must be abandoned. Poverty is a complex and multifaceted problem. Since it can be caused by deprivation in different areas, there are in reality different poverty profiles. The poor are, in fact, by no means a homogenous group. There is a multitude of different poverty groups with different interest and needs, such as women and children, the rural and the urban poor, members of various ethnic group and religious communities. This can lead not only to conflict between different poverty groups but also to discord within the respective groups, hampering the formulation of consistent strategies for reducing poverty.

Varieties of Poverty

If mass poverty is to be lastingly eliminated, its causes must be recognised and purposively eradicated. This is the only way to go beyond cosmetic treatment of the symptoms to provide permanent solutions. Poverty cannot be attributed to a single cause. It can always be traced back to the aggregation of various factors deriving to a large extent from the social system concerned. The divers contexts in which the production factors labour, capital and natural resources, technical knowledge, and the total environment relevant to development interact give birth to different "varieties of poverty". Successful projects and programmes for reducing poverty therefore require the fullest possible analysis of all the relevant elements and relationships of the concrete social system.

Other things being equal, the lower the percapita income of the population, the greater the extend of absolute poverty. Since this average income is in turn an indicator for the level of economic development, poverty can partially be explained in terms of the factors responsible for the economic underdevelopment of India. All strategies that contribute to improve the level of economic development can accordingly also provide an at least partial solution to the problem of poverty. In other words, a well-conceived development policy can at the same time be a functioning policy for reducing mass poverty as well.

Growth with Poverty

On the other side it has to be seen that economic growth is not automatically linked with poverty reduction. Historical examples of the last three decades clearly show that economic growth can go hand in hand with poverty increase. Even in cases where the above mentioned requirements of a development-promoting policy have been fulfilled, growth was accompanied by an increase in poverty due to a missing participation of broad segments of the population in this growth process. Or to formulate it more generally: Between growth and distributional justice—defined at least as reduction mass poverty—can be a target conflict which has to be solved by other measures than by additional growth politics. In fact, the more unequally income is distributed, the more probable material poverty becomes. The factors determining the interpersonal distribution structure of a country thus also contribute to explaining poverty.

For the mass of the poor, ownership of productive resources is usually limited to their own (mostly unskilled) labour. To a lesser extent they may also have property rights in land (e.g., in the case of very small scale farmers), and in material assets (e.g., simple implements). The level of education and training that determines human capital is, by contrast, usually so low that no marked improvements of their position can be expected. In most cases the poor of a society are also completely inadequately trained. With the exception of their labour, they thus dispose of no or of only very few productively utilisable resources. This is true for both the rural and the urban poor.

Their situation is made even more difficult by the fact that their resources can frequently not be used for farming or certain activities to be carried on despite adequate qualification, this can contribute just as much to poverty as repressive measures taken by big land-owners against small farmers, or the activities of criminal groups in poor urban areas. The utilisation of property rights can also be prevented by the complete absence of the additional resources (such as credits or jobs) required to carry on productive activities, or by their being available only on unacceptable conditions.

But even if the productively utilisable resources can actually be brought into use to produce goods and services, it is still not certain that an adequate level of income will be generated. At both the national and the international level, free entry to the market for the goods and services produced is not always attained. Since there are frequent legal, physical, and psychological barriers to entering the market. In some cases, certain groups are not permitted to sell in institutionally secured markets, or may do so only subject to severe restrictions in the national context, for example, ethnic minorities, adherents of certain religions, members of particular castes.

Without a doubt, the behaviour of individual groups and persons contributes to breeding or consolidating their own poverty. A decisive role is played by the relation between the culture-specific willingness to achieve, personal attitudes towards achievement and actual capacity for performance—always with reference to underlying components of poverty. However, the social systems concerned are likely to be of far greater significance in generating poverty. As a rule, the poor are a marginal group within a social system who do not participate in the political, social and economic decision-making and development processes. This marginality is not an isolated phenomenon. It is system-related and often the very rational reaction of the poor to discriminating framework conditions for their economic as well as non-economic behaviour. If the poor are not permanently to remain passive recipients of the alms of material aid, the marginalised population groups must integrated into the system. For this purpose, considerable structural and functional changes in the systems concerned are necessary, including a certain degree of redistribution of resources, of economic opportunities, and of political power in favour of the poor. The precondition for such changes is that the ruling elites realise that in the long run mass poverty must almost inevitably lead to revolution which in most cases generates dramatic losses also for the elites themselves.

The Poor Must Act

However, in India there is no or very little ability and willingness on the part of the socially dominant groups to carry out such changes to the system. Since for the foreseeable future the poor can expect no real support from the system that discriminates against them, the initiative for such changes—if one excludes the possibility of external intervention—must come from the poor themselves. They must learn to help themselves. Self-help is consequently a constituent element in poverty-oriented development strategies. Self-help measures of this sort should aim not only to improve the situation of the poor as such. They should also contribute to overall development by personal initiative. An awareness of making a real productive contribution to a society is an important factor in 'socio-psychological" demarginalisation. Such efforts at self-help should ideally develop within the group of the poor. Under the conditions prevailing in India, self-help must always be regarded as a group phenomenon and framed accordingly. Group successes generally provide the basis on which individuals gain greater opportunities to help themselves. If, however, the poor are unable to improve their situation by their own efforts, support for these efforts must be forthcoming. Such self-help support measures can be the object of a poverty-oriented development policy. They should most usefully not intervene at the level of the target group itself but indirectly, at that of self-help support institutions, so as to avoid stifling burgeoning self-initiative efforts.

Every form of community self-help requires the participation of its members. Participation is thus not only a development instrument, but also a goal in itself, since it gives people a sense of self-respect and belongings. It should thus be an essential component in any development strategy for reducing poverty. In contradiction to this demand, the poor are frequently treated more as objects than as subjects in the development process. The consequent lack of participation in the decision-making process can even be categorised as a primary cause of poverty. Indeed, as long as there is no genuine delegation of initiative, decision-making and implementation, democratisation will be no more than a slogan. If development is to be durable, it is essential to involve the marginalised groups in the planning and implementation of development programmes, and to give them a right of co-determination. This participation requires the poor to develop a critical awareness of their situation. They must stop accepting their poverty as more or less inevitable and adapting their behaviour to the situation. They must become conscious of their poverty and learn to regard it as deprivation. This critical awareness is the essential precondition for them being able to help themselves. Self-help and participation are thus inseparably interlinked.

Anti-poverty strategies directly addressing the target groups of the poor and which place no great value on self-help are doomed to failure in the long run. In the euphoric development policy conviction that help for self-help was the right way, it was, however, frequently overlooked that genuine self-help can only develop durably under certain minimum political, socio-cultural, institutional and economic conditions. If such "margins for action" do not exist, the spontaneous development of self-help rapidly falls victim to the pressure of vested interests.

Gradual Approach Needed

What goals a poverty-oriented development policy would have to adopt, what strategies in reducing poverty ought to be developed, or what strategies can be successful in given contexts all depend on the concrete form taken by the circumstances as has been addressed here. At any rate, modesty is called for in this respect. However, ambitious it may sound to attempt to formulate a comprehensive policy for reducing poverty, in reality a gradual approach is to be recommended. In most cases it is expedient to restrict initial efforts to reducing material poverty, especially since theoretical knowledge has made most progress in this field.

It should always be kept in mind that anti-poverty strategies have political implications, since in essence they always amount to the redistribution of resources and political power, and the reorganisation of institutions. The less evident the impression of a "zero-sum game", the greater will be the chances of prevailing an evolutionary development vis a vis the dominant society. From this point of view, poverty-oriented development policy is always a strategy of limited conflict, and is thus always caught between the desired evolution and the risk of revolution deteriorating into chaos that seldom improves the lot of the "poorest of the"poor.

17

Employment and Poverty Alleviation

Today the key socio-economic problem is large-scale unemployment. Spreading joblessness brings many other problems in its wake. It erodes national incomes and living standards, aggravating the already grindingly difficult job of promoting development and alleviating poverty. Joblessness also raises government budget deficits, increasing macro-economic instability while soaking up investment for productive capital expenditure, education, training and relief aid. And joblessness ruins lives and communities by depriving people of the dignity and satisfaction that comes with earning one's keep and making a contribution to the well-being of family and society.

Theories about how best to nurture development (and thus create jobs) have shifted considerably over the last decade. The state role has evolved, in the minds of many, from being a source of relief for the problems of unemployment, poverty and underdevelopment, to being a fundamental cause of these problems through the distorting impact of its intervention on the market.

However, the more market-oriented philosophy that grew up during the 1990s has yet to provide convincing solutions in practice at least not on a grand scale and especially not in terms of job creation as the present jobless economic recovery demonstrates.

The weakness of the current recovery and past approaches to economic development can be traced to the failure to consider employment as the predominant means of promoting growth and alleviating poverty. In policy circles it has too long been an almost ignored priority.

Current trends thus bode poorly, particularly as unemployment rates soar. In light of the circumstances, we need to begin re-examining some of the fundamental questions—if only to find out what has gone wrong with the answers.

Minimum Wage?

Let's begin with wages. With corporate restructuring in full force on a global scale, are low wage rates required to raise employment and maximise profits? A top manager of a multinational consumer electronics group certainly thinks so; he likened the perfect factory to a ship "so that we could move it around the world to where labour was cheapest". Perhaps, but this bottom-line emphasis on unit labour costs ignores at least two other factors; namely, that higher wages can act as a screen to select more productive workers and that higher wages translate into better productivity via improved worker nutrition, increased consumption and a generally healthier quality of life.

If higher wages being these benefits (and it is an open question) should government insist that there be a minimum wage rate? Neo-classical economists tend to respond "no", assuming that a higher wage rate puts money into the pockets of some low wage workers while forcing many others out of work because companies cannot afford to pay them.

Technology Transfer

The impact of technology is another area in need of study. Technological innovation is usually labour-saving and tends to originate in industrialised countries, moving toward developing countries like India, Pakistan where labour tends to be low cost and abundant. Would it therefore make sense to slow down or somehow restrict technology transfer, especially to development markets, in the interest of preserving employment?

The answer here is clearly—No. Historical evidence abundantly demonstrates that attempts to retard technological progress bring about greater poverty and lower growth. Technology, infact, is at the heart of the new endogenous growth theory which is very much in vogue among development economists today. Slowing down or inhibiting technology transfer would certainly dash many countries' development hopes and aggravate poverty. However, the relationship between technology, development, employment and poverty alleviation is not without its complications.

In the 1980s, the buzz word among development specialists was "appropriate technology", i.e., small-scale and labour-intensive technologies that would increase productive output while allowing an equilibrium solution to be found such that the ratio of the productivity of labour to that of capital is proportional to their relative prices. The conditions for this "small is beautiful" approach to technology tended to be best met in agricultural production. However, where manufacturing industry is concerned, the small-is-beautiful approach foundered badly when the only viable technological alternatives proved to be highly capital-intensive.

Development Gap

A wide gap has emerged between developing countries with an inward focus (which tended to be protectionist and pursue policies of import substitution) and those with an outward focus and a policy of pursuing export-led growth. Competing in international markets requires technology that is as good as or better than that found in advanced, industrialised nations. Small, therefore, is not beautiful in the global manufacturing economy where product standards are high and the elasticity of substitution between labour and capital is very limited.

The drive to obtain state-of-the-art technology thus leads to a policy conundrum: it is a pre-condition for success in manufactured exports, but the impulse to compete successfully in this most lucrative sector speeds up the transfer of technology from the developed to the developing world, thus reinforcing the bias toward labour saving equipment in developing countries and accelerating a process that is seen as a source of job loss in the industrialised countries.

Technology and Jobs

Before concluding that modern technology transfer is inimical to employment in developing countries, we have to distinguish clearly between technology's static and dynamic consequences. In a static sense, it is true that highly capital-intensive export industries may not create much employment on a net basis, but the dynamic effects of technology transfer do contribute to economic growth. And growth, in turn, generates multiplier effects in the form of demand, which stimulates ancillary production activities (like food processing or consumer goods) that rely on more labour-intensive technologies.

The problem is that the diffusion and application of technology on a global scale blurs the categories of international product specialisation and creates a much more competitive and conflict-prone international environment.

For example, we have already seen the Asian Tigers move from producing goods such as textiles and processed food to producing hi-tech and value-added consumer durables. This advance is only possible due to the growth of human capital (facilitated by investment and higher incomes) and it leaves production of textiles to other industrialising countries, like Indonesia, the Philippines and now China. But the dynamic comes at the expense of jobs in industrialised regions, like the US and the EC, which lost more than a quarter of their work force in textiles during the 1980s. In spite of job losses, advanced countries continue to produce textiles, notwithstanding major differences in the hourly wage rates for spinning and weaving and the fact that essentially the same hi-tech equipment is being used in most production centres.

Protectionism

What has happened in textiles is happening in other industrial sectors (automobiles, for example) as well. The intense market competition is providing to be a source of trade conflicts, and possibly protectionism, as jobs come under increasing pressure.

For many workers and managers, the benefits of foreign direct investment look increasingly like a zero-sum game for employment, and there is a real risk that the tenuous link between overall growth and employment will break down altogether. It is hardly surprising that we are already seeing negatively affected workers and local businesses clamouring for protection in advanced countries.

Governments Role

The concerned governments are suppose to carry out much of this research. The three initial lines of inquiry follow from three reasonable assumptions about the future.

- First, increase in welfare and consumption subsidies are out; investments in training and human capital are in. How can investments in human capital be directed to positive employment effects? Is it perhaps not time to explore more fully benefit schemes targeting the unemployed and the unskilled poor providing them with the type of subsidies that would enhance their human capital, improve their health and productivity through better nutrition and preventive medicine, and restore the dignity of holding a job?
- Second, given the quasi-inevitability of increased automation in manufacturing, how can other sectors (particularly agriculture and services) be developed to

export their long-term potential for employment creation?

- Third, given the inevitable pressures of work and productivity in the global economy, what sort of alternative institutional arrangements need to evolve with respect to industrial relations, employment and work conditions?

Finding answers to these and other questions will require no small amount of new thinking, but parochialism or a failure of imagination would be fatal flaws in this global era.

18

Can Economic Growth Reduce Poverty?

New Findings on Inequality, Economic Growth and Poverty

Many people still think first of 'economic growth' in relation to poverty reduction. Indeed, their correlation is one of the mot-discussed issues of combating poverty. The relationship is of great importance because if there is a clear causal dependency, reducing poverty could fundamentally be limited to measures to promote growth. However, if there was low growth or stagnation if would not be possible to reduce poverty decisively. In the opposite case, that of the phenomena having no causal relation, promising measures to reduce poverty could be taken up even without economic growth.

Hardly anyone now explicitly expresses the view that economic development trickles down automatically to the poor. Practical experience has refuted this assumption dating from the early days of development policy in the 1960s. However, a number of studies show development of growth and a decline in poverty running parallel. On the other hand, there are also examples which show that despite high economic growth, poverty is not reduced markedly. The common answer to the question this raises is thus: Yes, growth can reduce poverty, but only if additional measures oriented on the poor are taken up. This is often termed pro-poor-growth. But what that means in detail, and whether economic growth as such plays a causal role at all, is not clarified. It is worth taking a look at the arguments on the basis of more recent empirical and theoretical knowledge.

No Direct Causality Between Growth and Poverty Reduction

Among the many indicators of poverty, the income of the poor (income poverty) has the closest relationship to economic growth. An increase in gross domestic product and thus national income could, if other factors come into play be linked with an increase in the per capita income of the poor.

Such a relationship between economic growth and the income of the poor, however, cannot be described as causal, as is asserted implicitly time and again by the statement that growth is a necessary but not sufficient precondition for poverty reduction. In so far as growth and poverty reduction arise at the same time at the end of a process, they exist alongside each other. It would be almost a tautology to say that the former is the cause or part-cause of the latter. Both express the same thing, namely a change in per capita income as well, and both have similar causes. What matters is recognising what these causes are and what specific factors must come into play so that the income of the poor grows too. Growth as a "prerequisite" or "condition" is then no longer the focus; the priority is asking for specific policies that result in higher incomes for the poor. The detour in thinking about growth is not necessary. Since, however, it is based on similar factors, such as fiscal policy/budget structure, employment policy, combating inflation, and institutional development, economic growth can also emerge if poverty is reduced. The difference of views lies in the fact that under the heading 'poverty reduction' the aim is no longer growth, but a purposeful reduction of poverty.

Therefore, in reverse, successful combating of poverty can be seen as being the cause of growth insofar as activating the capabilities of the poor and using their productive capacity of the poor and using their productive capacity triggers economic drive.

Indirect Causality Between Growth and Poverty Reduction?

So even if economic growth fundamentally has no direct causal impact on poverty, growth still can reduce it indirectly. This is the case when due to positive economic development a government has greater revenue and uses the surplus for combating poverty, for example by providing such public goods as education and health services. Also in these cases, however, growth is not a compelling precondition. Even without growth greater government revenue can be achieved for example by more efficient tax collection. And leeway for social welfare spending can be gained by redistributing the budget, such as by cutting military appropriations. Furthermore, an automatic process is not given because the government can also use surplus funds for non-social purposes.

Creation of jobs due to increased economic activity can be another indirect link between economic growth and income poverty, if such a development generates income and reduces poverty. But also in this case I see no compelling causality because, for instance, industrial jobs are not necessarily open to the really poor. In addition, these positive impacts occur to a considerable extent only in the event of labour-intensive development. In many countries, however, economic growth is achieved by capital-intensive production.

Inequality, Growth and Income Poverty

If national incomes, grow, a naïve observer might assume that the income of the poor must also grow along with it. But that would be a statistical fallacy. Even if only the income of the rich grows, this results in macro-economics statistics showing a higher per capita income. What the true conditions are is shown as soon as one divides the population statistically into income groups, such as in fifths, as is usual. It then turns out that the bald figures on average per capita growth can certainly cloak a situation where the income of the richest fifth of the population is growing fast while that of the poorest fifth is stagnating. Despite growth, the gap between the two becomes even wider.

The unequal distribution of income (and of other assets such as property and access to social services), and its connection to poverty reduction and growth has recently returned to the forefront of the debate.

It is obvious that inequality and its changes have direct effects on the poverty situation. Does inequality also have an impact on poverty via its relation to growth, because growth promotes or reduces inequality? Earlier, the predominant view was that rapid growth was linked with at least a temporary increase in inequality, so that a distinct policy of growth initially disadvantaged the poor.

The current dominant view is that growth has no foreseeable effects on inequality and that inequality changes only very slowly, in reverse, however, it is assumed that greater equality is a determinant of growth. According to that view, an indirect relationship between poverty on one side and inequality as a factor dependent upon growth on the other is not given.

That leads to the conclusion that fair distribution has more weight than growth. Fair distribution, however, does not depend upon growth. An appropriate policy is possible at any time, not only after an economic situation has improved. The notion that still shimmers through the debate that "something must be earned first before it can be distributed", is wrong. It is a matter of designing policy and the entire economic process right from the start in such a way that the surplus benefits all including the poor. Important elements of such a policy are, for example, land reform and development of finance systems.

Relationship of Growth to Poverty

According to today's conventional wisdom, income poverty expresses only a part of what poverty means. Not least through the voices of the poor themselves, it has become clear that violation of human dignity and rights, a lack of participation in decisions and exclusion from society, unequal treatment of men and women, and vulnerability are also regarded as poverty. For poverty is caused to a great degree by conflicts of power and interests. Income poverty often is not even seen as the greatest problem.

What relationship do these more far reaching characteristics of poverty have to economic growth? A direct relationship of growth to socially-related aspects such as women's inheritance rights, land rights and exclusion from decisions cannot be seen. Considerable improvements in favour of the poor can be achieved here even without economic growth.

Those who see a strong and causal connection between economic growth and poverty reduction must ask themselves what the prospects are for high growth rates and thus for decline in poverty. Coupling poverty reduction to economic growth is problematic. If only low growth rates are to be expected.

Another question is whether continuous increases in growth are at all desirable and possible in the medium to long term. In this connection, a difference should perhaps be made between developing countries and industrialised nations. But environmental compatibility and availability of resources set limits to growth for both. Some academics assume that industrialised nations have already reached an inherent limit (stagnation theory) and that the high growth rates of earlier years will not return. Moreover, they add, full employment is no longer achievable due to, among other things, an ongoing increase in productivity, and current unemployment cannot be reduced by customary means. In any case, if growth were to be taken as the major benchmark, the prospects for a radical reduction of income poverty around the world would be modest.

Summing Up

Poverty is a complex problem and reducing it depends upon many interconnected factors that is why poverty cannot be attributed to one main cause nor its reduction based on one main strategy. Economic growth is just one strategic element among many others related to poverty reduction. An indirect causal connection between growth and poverty reduction can only be seen because governments will have a grater scope for action due to economic growth, and if they promote labour-intensive development.

Therefore growth's role in poverty reduction must be put into perspective Growth cannot be the first thing that comes to mind, nor is it the golden path to reducing poverty. The simplistic theory of economic growth as the main condition obstructs the bigger picture; it clings to the underlying and ongoing belief in the trickle-down effect. Even if there is no growth or for inherent reasons there can be none, there are promising ways to take on the challenge of mass poverty in the developing countries. Up front, governments and bilateral and multilateral donors must have the political will to design economic, financial and social policies so that they are oriented on poverty in a coherent way—the result can also be economic growth.

19

For Richer, For Fairer

Poverty Reduction and Income Distribution

Will the international target of reducing poverty by half over the next 15 years be met? Not unless growth efforts are accompanied by significant improvements in income distribution. Poverty reduction is a twin function of the rate of growth and of changes in income distribution. The research shows better distribution has as much impact on reducing poverty as had increased growth. And given predicted rates of economic growth, it emerges as the factor that will make the main difference between success and failure for new 'pro-poor' growth strategies.

Over the past decade, the amount of poverty reduction resulting from a given rate on economic growth has varied in close step with income distribution. On average, a growth rate of 10 per cent reduced the poverty headcount (the percentage of people living on less than $ 1 a day) by 9 per cent in countries where income was fairly equally distributed. However in countries where income was unequally distributed, a growth rate of 10 per cent reduced the poverty headcount by only 3 per cent.

The World Bank estimated that developing countries will grow at 4 per cent per capita per annum until 2015. So the good news is that the income-poverty target is attainable provided that significant improvements take place in income, distribution. These can be achieved ex-ante, by designing growth strategies that increase disproportionately the incomes of the poorest or ex-post, by redistributing income through taxation. Many questions arise. What is the recipe for income-redistributing growth? Is there a trade-off between growth and distribution? An ex-post strategies of reduction feasible? These questions are far from new. Indeed, to a large degree, they are the very questions on which the development studies profession is founded. Nevertheless, they have been neglected in recent years. Does current research offer new perspectives? Articles in this issue of insights offer six main conclusions. They are that:

- We need a way to measure 'pro-poor growth.' The concept originates from the 1990 World Development Report of the World Bank and is taken to mean a labour intensive growth path that encompasses the economic activities of the poor. However, such a growth path could be accompanied by increasing, declining or static income inequality. Mc Culloch and Baulch propose that the 'poverty bias of growth or PBG (whether pro poor or not) be defined by comparing actual change in income distribution with the change that would have resulted had all incomes grown at one rate with no change to income inequality. This difference is compared in their report (opposite) for two states in India. From this comparison it emerges that growth in Bihar State was accompanied by worsening income distribution and has been biased against the poor, whereas in Andhra Pradesh the reverese was true.

- Growth might be expected to be pro-poor if it takes place in areas and sectors where the poor live and work. For the poorest countries this means mostly in rural areas and to all large extent in agriculture. In Asia, Green Revolution technologies were adopted by poor farmers because they were scale-neutral and low-risk. Poor non-farmers also benefited from the extra employment and lower food prices that resulted. In Sub-Saharan Africa, the Green Revolution has been slower in coming, but research at Reading by Mosley suggests an African Green Revolution will help. In Uganda, for example, the spread of new technologies in maize and cassava has contributed to sharp falls in poverty, notable in the country's North where mosaic resistant cassava has made a conspicuous difference to farmer's yields and incomes in an otherwise poor and undeveloped region.

- Even so, as many will remember well from debates about the Green Revolution in Asia, not everybody benefits from growth. In Ethiopia, researchers from the Universities of Oxford and Addis Ababa found that rural poverty has fallen sharply since the change of government in 1992, driven by market liberalisation and better weather (see Dercon, backfold). Yet those who have gained have been those with assets, including land, oxen for ploughing, edcuation and access to public goods such as roads. Those without assets are left behind. Rural inequality has actually risen, implying Ethiopia could reduce poverty faster if policies countered inequality yet maintained current growth rates.

- People without assets might be expected to compensate by migrating or moving out of agriculture. Sometimes this happens, but seeking off-farm opportunities may be easier of the haves tan the have-nots. In rural Zimbabwe, for example, Piesse and Thirtle have shown that (in more remote areas at least) those with higher farm incomes are better placed to exploit off-farm opportunities, including the option of working in town.

- In any case, migration to town may not offer much to the unskilled—again, a problem facing those without assets. The evidence here comes from China, in research carried out by the institute of Economics and Statistics. Wage employment has increased in urban China, but wage inequality has increased sharply, with falling real wages for the unskilled.

- The efficiency (hence the growth) and equity trade-off is far from clear cut. Analysis by Knight of the reasons behind rising wage-income inequality in China has revealed that some of these changes reflect greater labour market efficiency. In other words, more productive, experienced and skilled worker have become better paid. Other changes hint a new inefficiencies creeping into China's labour market, such as growing labour market, such as growing discrimination: females and minority groups find they are disadvantaged in the labour market, whereas members of the Communist Party are more likely to get jobs. Other signs are sharper segmentation, with state employees paid more than private sector counterparts and growing differences in wage rates between the provinces, not offset by labour mobility.

The cross-section of findings offered in these pages does not amount to a systematic review of the inequality question' in developing countries. Far from it: here is fertile ground for further research. Even so, we are confident that it is time to promote inequality to the fore of the research and policy agenda.

20

Taking a Lead in the Fight Against Poverty?

World Bank and IMF Speed Implementation of their New Strategy

A change in development policy strategy in the poorest countries is at present being prepared with incredible speed. The IMF-style structural adjustment programmes that have been criticised for many years are being scrapped. The countries are now to take their own decisions on their paths to development. Their governments will no longer formulate poverty reduction programmes top-down, but in an intensive and long-term dialogue with societal groups and organisations. Governments and institutions of the North commit themselves to supporting these processes, such as by debt relief on an unprecedented scale. Dream or reality?

New Strategy Paper

Behind this euphoria lines a new abbreviation, PRSP, standing for Poverty Reduction Strategy Paper, which the IMF and World Bank invented last year. The G-7 countries in Cologne not only announced debt relief for the heavily indebted poor countries (HIPCs) but also demanded that it must serve above all for poverty reduction. The PRSP concept was then presented at the annual conference of the two Bretton Woods organisations.

The most important principles of the new "super weapon" in the fight against poverty are:

- PRSPs are papers, which describe the medium-term development paths of the poorest countries of the South, particularly their strategies to combat poverty, and by this means enlist international support. A PRSP is not only the prerequisite for granting debt forgiveness in the context of the HIPC initiative. It is also necessary for all new IMF and World Bank loans to the so-called IDA countries, the some 70 poorest countries that receive concessional loans from the World Bank's International Development Agency (IDA). According to the World Bank, PRSPs should also be required for all future pledges of bilateral development assistance.

- Not only social sector programmes, but also the economic and financial policies of the developing countries are in future to be aimed at fighting poverty. Previously, the IMF always pronounced that a growth-oriented national economy and a far-reaching integration in the world market would have a trickle-down effect and also benefit the poor. Now the poor are to be asked what policies can help materially to improve their situation.

- PRSPs are to be developed on the basis of self-responsible country ownership. Accordingly, development and structural adjustment strategies are no longer to be developed by the Washington finance institutions, but the countries themselves.

- The heading "country ownership" is to underline that not only governments are called upon, PRSPs should come into being in a participatory process. That means involvement of trade unions, NGOs cooperatives, associations, grassroots groups, political parties and parliaments. A country's PRSP should be developed in a societal debate, a dialogue between governments on one side and parliamentary, private sector and civil society on the other.

Rhetoric or Reality?

Are PRSPs the expression of a change of paradigm? In brief, if all what the papers contain is implemented in a consistent and wide-ranging, way, the chances of achieving it are good but there are a number of open questions. The answers to them will have a bearing on success or failure.

Is the IMF really changing its policy on the poorest countries or merely wrapping its old policy in new words? The growing criticise of the IMF in recent years strengthened latterly by the evaluation of the ESAF (Enhanced Structural Adjustment Facility) programmes, which once again proved their blatant weaknesses called for reaction and is now triggeringchanges --real or only rhetorical? There will be no more old-style ESAF loans based on macro-economic structural adjustment programmes. But the credit line remains, and is now called the Poverty Reduction and Growth Facility (PRGF). This will be granted on the basis of the PRSPs, which in each case must also be accepted by the IMF board of directors. How much influence will the IMF have on the design of the PRSPs? What happens if a government choose macro-economic strategies combat poverty which go against previous IMF policy? Open questions. Moreover, there is still no answer to the question of why the IMF is at al coming on with long-term and low-interest lines of credit in the poorest countries.

Mixed Feelings with Regard to World Bank Role

- Will the World Bank use the PRSP process to expand its own institutional power further? NGOs in the North and South are viewing this with mixed feelings. Many welcome the fact that for the moment the World Bank appears to be asserting itself against its twin, the IMF. On the other hand, 50 years of experience with World Bank strategies have certainly not strengthened their trust in the Bank's ability to make a convincing fight against poverty. That is why the EURODAD network also questions the role of the World Bank (and the IMF) in the PRSP process. It says the papers should not be presented to the two financial institutions, whose power over the development strategies of countries of the South thus would increase further. Rather, PRSPs should for example, be laid before a Round Table of all donors chaired by the United Nations Development Programme (UNDP).

Ownership

- The principles of developing countries being responsible for their own development strategies are as old as it is—in theory—right. There have been frequent complaints about shortcomings in ownership. But now, after decades of development strategies being set and structural adjustment programmes being dictated from outside, the governments of the poorest countries, which in many cases have only weak institutional capacities, can hardly taken on sole respnsibility overnight. In addition, of course, not a few of the countries are ruled by corrupt political elites (promoted from outside over decades) that give little reason to hope they would immediately switch to poverty reduction polities. Scepticism and critical observation is justified even if there is no alternative to governments of the south taking over greater responsibility.

- Civil society actors are now asked to help out in particular in those countries whose governments appear to be less trustwothy. A nice idea that has little to do with real life. Civil society actors in developing countries in general and in the poorest countries in particular are extraordinarily weak institutions which in many cases are totally dependent on financing from the North.

- The civil society landscape in other countries is even weaker. However, social actors in many countries could make useful contributions to developing sustainable strategies. But that calls for meaningful and lasting support, including financial support, capacity-building, and in some countries also political pressure to gain scope for societal engagement.

It is reasonable that not only the World Bank and other official donors but also, and above all, the northern NGO partners of these actors are now giving much thought to how civil societies in the south can be strengthened.

Participation?

Even assuming there were civil society actors capable of dialogue, that does not clarify what participation in the PRSP process is really supposed to mean. Is civil society only to be listened to, or can it if necessary refuse to approve a PRSP? What impact would have on acceptance of the document by the IMF and World Bank and other donor? And in view of the great time pressure, will civil society be at all able to formulate discuss and feed their positions into the process? It could be of decisive importance for the current debate on the PRSP model to delink the urgently needed debt relief from drawing up a PRSP programme, which simply needs more time. For example, it is conceivable that there would be no great problems in granting a country a moratorium on debt servicing so long as a PRSP process is continuing and then for giving debt when it is completed. That would ease the time problem for NGOs and at the same time maintain pressure on governments actually to arrive at poverty reduction strategies that were developed in a participatory process.

Other Causes of Poverty in Developing Countries

The entire current process is focused on the countries of the south, their governments and societies. That diverts attention from the responsibility of the donors and creditors. Not only that the IMF's structural adjustment programmes to date have been counterproductive for fighting poverty (why does the IMF not admit that openly just for Once?) Not only that the now promised debt reliefs are coming much too late the debt crisis of the poorest countries was deplored decades ago!). The present strategy also ignore various other exogenous causes of poverty in the South. What impacts do the finance and trade policies of northern countries have on the modest attempts to enable sustainable development in the South? What consequences will the continuing cutting of development budgets have on the South (no one anyway ventures to talk nowadays about the old 0.7 per cent ODA-GNP ratio) Fort the donors and creditors to now pass the buck of sole responsibility to the governments of the South and present themselves in the background as noble do-gooders may be a successful strategy in terms of domestic politics, but not an acceptable one for development policy.

21

Unemployment in the Poor and Rich Worlds

Different Causes, but Converging Policies?

In view of the magnitude of global unemployment, all the customary formulas offered by economists against mass unemployment—the basic socio-economic problem of modern times—appear to be quackery. Neither quantitative, nor any kin of 'qualitative', growth will be able to eliminate the disastrous worldwide lack of jobs. For ecological reasons it is impossible to include 800 million or more unemployed in the production process through corresponding growth. The resulting increase in global Gross Domestic Product would require consumption of natural resources, energy and the environment which, given even the greatest possible productivity in those sectors, could not even be sustained for two or three decades.

In addition, aiming to achieve full employment through growth will be even more difficult even in the rich economies. For it is most likely that work productivity will continue to rise worldwide. Countries such as China, which are in the initial phase of modernisation, are still producing at a relatively still low productivity rate. But that is precisely why they can achieve notable increases in productivity in a short time by importing technology from highly-developed countries. The advantage of rapid 'catch-up rationalisation', however, is being bought at the cost of rising unemployment and progressive impoverishment.

Employment through Redistribution of Work

The notion that jobs can at some time be created for 800-900 million unemployed who will work 35 or even 40 hours a week at the productivity level of the highly-developed countries of four or five decades ago is absurd. The only realistic possibility of eliminating the world's unemployment problem is by far-reaching redistribution of work and income. The change needed for that demands fundamentally new concepts of prosperity: a reflection on the philosophy of the 'life of happiness'. 'New concepts of prosperity' means that technological progress would no longer be used mainly to deliver rising per capita income and excessive consumption. Instead, given a sufficient material standard of living, the quality of life would be improved primarily by shortening working hours. It is about, so to speak, assigning instrumental good sense new goals. Plus reshaping socio-economic conditions in such a way that the politicians will again be compelled to orient themselves on the good of the community and humanistic values instead of filling the pockets of the wealthy. It is sheer ideology, although very persuasive, to cite 'globalisation' and its alleged 'iron laws' in defaming the welfare state, full employment and social justice as out-of-date wishful thinking. A return to the state-guided social competitive system as practised during the first decades after the Second World War is possible just as it was politically feasible to make the transition from the old order of unfettered, ruthless capitalism to the mixed economies of the social market economy types. So it is a matter of restoring the proven structures of a mixed economic system.

However, in contrast to the first postwar decades it is now not sufficient to regenerate nation-sate interventionism. Appropriate international regualtions are required. Above all, it will depend upon reversing the new laissez-faire developments in international economic relationships which today are subsumed under the buzzword 'globalisation'. That is, to oppose over-liberalisation and its disastrous social and inhuman impacts. It will depend on the broad mobilisation of the losers in the process of globalisation whether the necessary fundamental change of course can still be made in time before a catastrophe. In particular, the new myth must be opposed that declares globalisation as a kind of law of nature and thus suggests resignation and adaptation to an allegedly unavoidable process of destruction of social and human achievements.

Mass Unemployment in the Poor Economies

The employment problems in the rich and the poor hemispheres differ not only in their magnitude, but also in their causes. The wretched condition of the poor economies is due above all to historical reasons: colonialism and, in the post-colonial era, the constraints to independent development imposed by the hegemonic influence of the rich industrial states. The waste of scarce resources by international and civil wars, and the dictatorships with their upperclass luxury consumption and inefficient, thus development obstructing exploitation structures often supported by the industrialised nations have for a long time repressed and in many cases destroyed autonomous development potential. The colonial and post-colonial distortion also contributed at least indirectly to the current population problems of the poor countries. The politically inflicted mass poverty and under-development stabilised or in fact brought about economic, socio-psychological and ideological mechanisms which oppose an effective population policy. As we know, the average educational level in many developing countries, especially among women, is too low to give a modern population policy a chance of success. Mass unemployment in the poor countries is the result of poverty. In this respect, it is about a production-side problem: to few resources, to little real and human capital, and the inefficient, unproductive use of much of the anyway limited added value of society. The picture is totally different in the rich countries the over-production economies.

Unemployment in Over-Production Systems

The main cause of mass unemployment in the industrialised nations has nothing to do with shortages. It is a phenomenon of surplus. Greater possibilities of production can no longer be used 'sufficiently profitably because the required demand is lacking. Production is done for profit. The necessary collateral condition is the satisfying of consumer needs. Employment is not even such a condition, but only a side effect which lapses immediately when labour-free production is technically possible. Thus, national income must be shared among wages and profits (or income from property). Profit is the difference between earnings and costs. Earnings depend upon demand. Macro-economic costs consist mainly of wages and salaries (including social security contributions). These definitive connections mean that profit can be made only if overall demand is greater than the total cost labour. But in the final analysis this demand can only come from the profit-earners themselves. In his book, a Treatise on Money, Keynes described this nexus as the theory of the Widow's cruse. Under capitalistic conditions, labour is only sought or hired if profit can be earned with it. But as making a profit depends upon the demand for consumption and investment by the shareholders, it can be seen that the degree of employment is determined by the demand behaviour of the class that receives income from property. In this respect, the widespread belief that greater investment also leads to more employment, namely via the effect of investment in demand, is right.

Lower Wages Mean Lower Demand

The lower the level of wages, and given an unchanged total demand, the greater are the profits that can be made. But it is more likely that in the case of falling wages the overall demand will also drop. For stabilising total demand would require the recipients of income from property to increase their spending on consumption and/or investment to the degree to which wages and the consumption based on them fell.

During the last 10 to 15 years the development of profits in most industrialised nations has been very favourable. But profits would have grown more strongly if the demand of the shareholder had been much greater. This would have created more employment at the same time. Thus, it can be assumed that the profits are simply too high for the shareholders to be able to go in for meaningful consumption or make profitable investments. That is the reason for the extreme redirection of capital from fixed assets to portfolio investment. The growth of speculative (unproductive) financial transactions during the 1980s and 1990s (buzzword: casino capitalism), corresponded with a relatively weak formations of real capital.

Wage rises, of course, narrows the scope for profit. But precisely this effect stimulated efforts to improve the profit situation not only by investment in rationalisation, but also by investment in expansion aimed at the growing mass purchasing power. Since more is being invested, the profit mass also is growing according to the principle of the Widow's cruse. Too low wages, as it were, relieve the shareholders of the pressure to innovate and invest and allow them to earn their profits too easily. That is the real message of the 'purchasing power theory' of wages.

Over-Accumulation and Under-Consumption

Overproduction has two different causes which, however, mostly occur in tandem. They are over-investment, or creation of over-capacities, on the one hand, and lack of demand due to relative saturation and an absence of mass purchasing power on the other. But the main reason for mass unemployment in the rich hemisphere currently lies on the demand side. During the first three decades after the Second World War supply and demand rose in relative balance. Economic fluctuations showed up as temporary declines in generally positive GDP growth rates. These decades of (dynamic) balance of growth are often described today as the era of 'Fordism'. Its essential feature is that rising wages ensure continuing growth of consumption, so that equally growing profits also flow relatively continuously into investments to expand capacity and create jobs. The label

'Fordism' expresses the 'simple' view of the theory for the buying power of wages which is said to have been propagated by Henry Ford I. This was that his workers should earn enough to be able to buy the cars they made.

The astonishingly balanced development of supply and demand from 1950 to the mid-1970s was due above all to postwar reconstruction and the pent-up demand of consumers who were starved by wartime economy shortages. This stimulated positive investment sentiment, and high investments brought at the same time high profits. The postwar growth that led within a short time to full employment was also linked with growth in productivity, which on multi-year average was more than twice that of the crisis period of the last 25 years. Thus, the so-called employment threshold (the GDP growth rate point at which employment growth begins) was much higher in those days than it is now, although there was full employment over a longer period. This simple fact opposes the thesis often propounded today that mass unemployment is above all related to rationalisation. Its is not rationalisation per se, that is, progress that boosts productivity, which is the evil. The problem is that the mistakes in distribution in supply are rooted in capitalistic structures result in increases in supply encountering insufficient demand for goods, whereby the demand for labour drops. However, the fact that demand policy contradicts the requirements of a social ethic that is ecologically responsible and right for the interests of the poor countries was already spelled out. So if a demand-oriented growth policy is practised at all, it should be designed to be as environmentally compatible as possible. After all, there are possibilities for that, such as by expanding the production of services that spares resources. A one-hour driving lesson costs more energy than one hour of ballet instruction.

The politically initiated and implemented over-liberalisation and surrender of social prosperity to global competition since the 1970s, which reproduces the old self-destructive mechanism of laissez faire, have during the last two decades markedly accelerated the crisis development inhere not in the system.

Summing Up, it is Noted that

- Full employments in the rich economies would certainly be possible by means of demand policy, but only at a high cost to the environment that is concomitant with high growth rates;
- The growth policy of the rich countries impairs the poor economies' possibilities of medium to long-term growth, since these are falling back ever further in the competition for ever scarcer and thus ever more expensive resources;
- The environmental collapse currently expected for the third or fourth generation after us, which obviously also will trigger a collapse of the world economy and—probably ahead of that-armed conflicts which today are hardly imaginable, would happen very much sooner if economic growth were to be increased to such a degree that it would bring full employment worldwide;
- In the long term, the problem of global unemployment and global poverty can only be solved by a policy of massive redistribution, and in fact a redistribution of work and income, whereby increases in productivity must be used mainly or only for shortening working hours. That is a demand, which appears to be utopian. But utopias of today often have the quality of scripting the reality of tomorrow.

22

Resistance to Change

Why Poverty Reduction Programmes Did Not Work

Poverty reduction as an overall objective of the global development industry is not new. The only problem is that so far it has not really worked. Despite several decades of economic growth and huge development aid disbursements, the number of countries the United Nations calls "least developed" (those with a per capita income of less than US$ 900 a year) has in fact nearly doubled since 1971, from 25 to 49. In the last decade (1990-2000) and despite all development efforts—not even one country was able to graduate from this group to a higher income level, may be with the exception of Botswana.

Meanwhile, poverty reduction has generated its own history. This programme has covered a wide range of approaches starting from the World Banks's small-farmers-strategies in the 1970s via the costly structural adjustment policies of the 1980s to the recent poverty reduction strategies of the 1990s Once more, the next development decade (2000-2010) has written "Attacking Poverty" on its banner. It seems that something must have gone wrong along the way. What (bitter?) lessons have been learnt from previous experience? Have they been factored into the new set of policies? Were there possibly some fundamental flaws which were overlooked, and can better results be expected during the next period? Or do the many failures and disappointments demonstrate that there is some systemic "resistance to change" by those in power in the least developed countries and perhaps also by the poor themselves?

1. What Can the Rural Poor Really Expect from Poverty Reduction Programmes?

In India, of example, 70 per cent of the people still earn their livelihood in the agricultural sector; most of the poor among them live in a kind of rural subsistence economy. People who live in a subsistence economy are naturally conservative. They are busy securing their survival and are very reluctant to take risks. Their living standard is measured in amounts of rice harvested; their wealth is measured in numbers of livestock. Within this simple framework, poor peasants behave very rationally. For example, a shift from food crops to cash crops, such as from rice to coffee or tapioca, would immediately endanger their subsistence in case of failure. Furthermore, the poor do not have the knowledge and skills to change their crops quickly in response to market demands. Moving from a subsistence economy to a commodity economy is therefore a big step for small farmers.

However, poor people are always happy to receive handouts from the Government like fertiliser, seeds, medicine or blankets. Roads, bridges and schools are also very welcome. Who would refuse a gift? From their point of view, it is the responsibility of the Government to distribute goods and services in the form of aid programmes as a way to share some of the prosperity of the city people with them. Nevertheless, as they see no direct and immediate benefit for themselves, they tend to take a rather passive attitude to change. Development workers have often complained about this common apathy and about the lack of will among the poor themselves to improve their situation. In the final analysis, rural development is more a problem of providing the right economic incentives for change than of overcoming traditional thinking and a conservative attitude.

2. What Kind of Incentives are Necessary to Achieve Increased Production in the Countryside?

In most poor countries the key to rural development is the problem of land ownership rights and of legal security. As long as people do not own the land that they cultivate, they are not interested in making any investments, be they in the form of labour or capital. Once a farmer has an ownership title and considers the land as his own, he will refrain from overusing the soil but shift crops and plant new trees. Moreover, he can then use his land as collateral for credits or even sell it and buy land somewhere else.

In addition to clear and irrevocable ownership rights, the rule of law is another crucial factor for development. People must feel safe from abuse of power by local elites and corrupt government officials. They must be able to enforce their basic rights in an impartial court of law. Furthermore, they must be safe from land expropriation without adequate compensation and from resettlement against their will. In other words, it is primarily their very stake holdership in the rural economy that will motivate them to increase their production. Of course, the other necessary incentives are access to markets, a fair price for their products and the availability of goods and services.

3. Poverty Reduction Programmes, if Not Accompanied by Parallel Institutional Reforms, Run the Risk of Creating a Modern Version of the Cargo Cult

Cargo cults spread during World War II in the highlands of Papua New Guinea at a time when several US cargo planes loaded with food supplies crashed into the hills. Suddenly, the native people could enjoy an abundant amount of goods, which literally fell down on them like a "gift from heaven". In the hope of attracting some more of these "silvery birds", the local hill-tribes constructed primitive models of airplanes, sat around them in a circle, and prayed that more "cargo" would drop on their territory. As this happened in some areas (albeit as a result of the air battle between Japan and the USA), it strengthened the belief in the cargo cult as some magical way to overcome poverty, at least for a short time.

There is a high risk that aid programmes under the banner of poverty reduction will create new "cargo cults" in the 49 least developed countries if they continue to carry out their "business as usual" and do not put strong emphasis on the rule of law and civil rights. Unfortunately, the setting up of reliable legal and social institutions in poor countries (which often seems to be the "software" of the development industry accompanying disbursements) is, in fact, as decades of experience have shown, the hard part of the process. But it is also indispensable for achieving any tangible results.

Why have there been until now only modest results in the areas of land reform, rule of law and the guarantee of basic civil rights? Why have people's participation and people's ownership as a strategy hardly taken root at all in the least developed countries? The answer must be sought in the role of powerful local groups and their vested interest, who obviously benefit from the prevailing status quo and a loose legal environment. A cargo cult promises bounty for all recipients; poverty reduction, however, means changing the rural power structure, too.

Conclusion

To insist on the rule of law, on people's participation in the development process, and on transparency and accountability, is again nothing new. Good political and administrative institutions go hand in hand with economic growth. The potential of economic development is quite limited if it works in a framework of social undevelopment and official indifference. Again the question is, who has so little been achieved in this field during previous decades? Was it the wrong medicine and why were the poor results of the aid programmes so carefully ignored by the international donor community?

Looking at the political systems of the 49 least developed countries, it is obvious that most of these countries are "more democratic in principle than in practice". Many of them are ruled by military or civil authoritarian regimes which are more used to giving orders than to listening to the grievances of the poor, Other governments, such as India, are "genuinely democratic at most levels but have historically found it difficult that political accountability reaches all levels of decision-making, particularly for the poor."

To sum up, it seems that resistance to change is equally shared by the cumbersome and often incompetent bureaucracies of the poor countries and the equally cumbersome international donor community, which has so far conveniently kept the call for more rural democracy and people's rights on the backburner. The major reason for the reluctance of the donor community to pursue the battle for the rule of law and the fight against endemic corruption was to avoid massive political confrontation with the receiver countries.

Would it not have been better to create proper incentives for the performance of poor countries, namely by halting loans to nations that do not manage their economies and their reform commitments effectively and increasing financial and technical support to those that do? The next decade will show how determined both local governments and donors are to tackle these problems for the sake of a better future.

23

Link Between Disability and Poverty

Disability affects nearly every fifth household in developing countries and is a prevalent contributing factor to family poverty.

An already poor household has an added financial burden when a disabled family member is not involved in productive activities. In the context of extreme poverty, a disability may sometimes turn into an asset when the person uses begging as a way to bolster the family income. But this is a degrading path that does not lead out of poverty.

What aggravates the situation is the fact that poverty is identified as one of the main causes of disability. This is especially so for those at the lowest strata of society who live in precarious conditions without education, hygiene and health care.

An important element of measures aimed at families living in absolute poverty is that they learn how to prevent disability. They must also learn that a disabled family member can take part in economic activities.

Increasing the economic usefulness of a disabled household member can help to reduce the poverty of many families. The income earned by the disabled person not only benefits him or her but the entire household as well.

However, anti-poverty strategies which target disabled household members without attempting to alleviate general household poverty would likely be futile.

One widespread misconception is that disabled people are unable to earn a living and to be self-reliant. As a consequence, disabled people are often targeted only for passives measure of income replacement and social welfare schemes. Active measures of income replacement and social welfare schemes. Active measure in their favour are conceived of as social activities and not economically relevant. Such misconceptions generate and reinforce exclusion, which in turn perpetuates poverty.

This highlights a dimension of poverty often overlooked by economists. They defined poverty only in terms of household income. But poverty also means to lack social status and to lose human dignity.

Thus, a basic criterion for an anti-poverty strategy at the micro-level is whether it serves to establish human dignity. An approach, which merely dishes out state subsidies or international aid to the destitute keeps the recipients in a position of dependence.

Targeting specific groups for poverty alleviation measures is always a highly sensitive issue. It can damage the fragile social fabric and may result in greater poverty for some while favouring others. Such a risk may be avoided through a participatory approach, which actively involves the poor and assists them in their efforts to gain control over their lives.

Disabled people are more likely to be poorer than their non-disabled peers because of the discrimination, which accompanies disability, not because of the impairment itself.

They suffer from social exclusion and frequently find themselves trapped in a web of neglect. The problem is even more acute for disabled women, who encounter enormous prejudices and obstacles in their quest to participate in social and economic life.

A more enlightened society will seek to integrate disabled people, to give them opportunities to learn and to work as others do. It will adjust the physical environment to accommodate their special needs.

This planet belongs to all people. If some people are trapped somewhere, we must all come forward to remove the causes of their discomfort. At the same time we must leave our shores open for anybody who decides to join us, or any body who decides to part our company.

Poverty denies a person control over his destiny. Poverty means not being able to tell what tommorrow would be like. If we examine the situation carefully we will see that the poverty is neighter created by the poor, nor sustained by the poor. It is the system of policies and institutions that we have built around us that creates and sustains poverty. Poverty is the denial of human rights. Over one billion people live below the absolute poverty line right now on this planet are denied of almost all human rights. There is no way one can defend the existence of poverty anywhere. Poverty is a disgrace for the entire man—kind Because we allow another humanbeing to die of hunger, or malnutrition, or common curable diseases, or exposure to climate, we are reduced to less human beings. If a particular world system is responsible for creating this massive poverty we must act to replace it.

Resource-wise or technology-wise, there is no reason why poverty should exist and continue to deepen and widen. If we make up our minds to wipe out poverty from the surface of the earth, the worst aspect of poverty can be removed within the next couple of decades.

Each human being is a wonderful creation of the creator. Each humabeing is born with great potentials. Poverty denies any opportunity for a person to achieve any of his/her potential. We have built a world system which is in the habit of pushing people down not building them up. It creates barriers around individuals, rather than remove them.

The most effective step that we must take to remove poverty is to create a system which creates enabling conditions for people and removes the existing barriers. The institutional barriers were skillfully crafted over the centuries to benefit a handful of people.

Resource-poor nations with high incidence of poverty waste away enormous human capability each day by denying poor people the use of their energy and ingenuity. If they could have been made economically active, not only they could have contributed in the national production, they would have helped expand the domestic market for the products produced. The disabled one can be transformed into the engine of grwoth if we only allow them to unleash their capacity.

We cannot be at peace with ourselves if we know there is a human being who lives a life worse than an animal. A human being is supposed to live differently than an animal. He/She is supposed to live a life with human dignity. Human dignity is what distinguishes a human being from an animal. When we cannot ensure this dignity for others, our own dignity becomes an empty pretense.

There must be a thousand and one ways to remove poverty from the earth. We may or may not know some of those ways already. Obviously there are many more ways yet to be designed, each more effectively than others. When we shall find them, how many of them we shall find, how quickly we find them will depend on how eager we are to find them. But to say that poverty cannot be overcome, directly and quickly, is to underestimate the capacity of human mind.

24

Peace and Poverty

Peace should not be understood in military terms, like absence of armed conflicts. Peace should be understood in a human way in a broad social, political and economic way. Peace should mean social justice between nations and within nations. It should mean establishment of human rights for all people.

In the new context the concept of "peace" would be the existence of a political and economic environment where each individual human being is truly free; free from the control of any powerful person or any powerful nation, free from poverty, hunger and indignities, each individual human being free to explore the limits of one's own potential.

Today peace is threatened, more than anything else, by poverty, unjust social and economic order, absence of democracy and environmental degradation.

The cold war cloud has gone. You can feel the breath of fresh air around the world. Now there is no visible competitor left for capitalism. It is quite risky to live with a philosophy, which has no challenger. To be safe, we must go to the essence of the philosophy of capitalism rather than be satisfied with the practices, which emerged over years through patchworks of expediency.

Contrary to common belief, it is not the "free enterprise" which is the essence of capitalism. It is the freedom of individual thought and freedom of individual action, which is the essence of capitalism. It is these freedoms, which support free enterprise, free trade, free circulation of capital, and free circulation of people.

We must work out a new system, appropriate for the new world, from the basics of capitalism, not from the practices of capitalism. Many of these practices take away freedom, rather than guarantee it. Traps must go. People cannot remain trapped in places where they cannot live because of ecological, political, or economic reasons. This planet belongs to all people. If some people are trapped somewhere, we must all come forward to remove the causes of their discomfort. At the same time we must leave our shores open for anybody who decides to join us, or anybody who decides to part our company.

Poverty denies a person control over his destiny. Poverty means not being able to tell what tomorrow would be like. If we examine the situation carefully we'll see that the poverty is neither created by the poor, nor sustained by the poor. It is the system of policies and institutions that we have built around us that creates and sustains poverty. Poverty is the denial of human rights. Over one billion people live below the absolute poverty line right now on this planet, are denied of almost all human rights. There is no way one can defend the existence of poverty anywhere. Poverty is a disgrace for the entire man-kind. Because we allow another human being to die of hunger, or malnutrition, or common curable diseases, or exposure to climate, we are reduced to less human being. If a particular world system is responsible for creating this massive poverty we must act to replace it.

Resource-wise or technology-wise, there is no reason why poverty should exist and continue to deepen and widen. If we make up our minds to wipe out poverty from the surface of the earth, the worst aspect of poverty can be removed within the next couple of decades.

We can build a poverty-free world at a fraction of the cost of what we spend on war preparations. Nations become very generous when it comes to making their war-machine heftier in the name of ensuring "peace". Can we persuade ourselves to allocate a part of our time, money and intellect to achieve peace by making the people at the bottom the winners, rather than nations winning wars? "Peace" achieved by winning wars is earned by destroying people. The real peace can be achieved by building people, by reinforcing people, by helping people to reach their potential. Removing poverty is the process of building people.

Each human being is a wonderful creation of the Creator. Each human being is born with great potentials. Poverty denies any opportunity for a person to achieve any of his/her potential. We have built a world system, which is in the habit of pushing people down not building them up. It creates barriers around individuals, rather than remove them.

The most effective step that we must take to remove poverty is to create a system, which creates enabling conditions for people and removes the existing barriers. The institutional barriers were skilfully crafted over the centuries to benefit a handful of people.

Resource-poor nations with high incidence of poverty waste away enormous human capability each day by denying poor people the use of their energy and ingenuity. If they could have been made economically active, not only they could have contributed in the national production, they would have helped expand the domestic market for the products produced. The poor can be transformed into the engine of growth if we only allow them to unleash their capacity.

We cannot be at peace with ourselves if we know there is a human being who lives a life worse than an animal. A human being is supposed to live differently than an animal. He/she is supposed to live a life with human dignity. Human dignity is what distinguishes a human being from an animal.

When we cannot ensure this dignity for others, our own dignity becomes an empty pretence.

There must be a thousand and one ways to remove poverty from the earth. We may or may not know some of those ways already. Obviously there are many more ways yet to be designed, each more effectively than others. When we shall find them, how many of them we shall find, how quickly we find them; will depend on how eager we are to find them. But to say that poverty cannot be overcome, directly and quickly, is to underestimate the capacity of human mind.

Poverty is homogeneous only when considered from the point of view of income or consumption: the uniformity of the poor as a category exists only on the level of the fact that they have little to consume. When considered from the point of view of production, i.e., the circumstances in which the poor must operate to gain their income, the conditions of poverty are extraordinary diverse. A concrete grasp of these diverse circumstances is the first step in developing relevant instruments to address not only the problems of the poor, but also the challenge of taking advantage of the opportunities available to them.

The conventional means of measuring economic progress, such as Gross National Product per capita, tell us little about the real nature of poverty. In recent years this sort of yardstick has been supplemented by measurements of food security, income distribution, and social development (encompassing health and education). These offer the possibility of composite indices, allowing the development of more rounded characterisations and comparisons of poverty at the national level. However, these principally refer to the symptoms of poverty, not to the relational factors generating it. Poverty is not a state of being; it is the effect of dynamic processes. While it is important to know where poverty is greatest, it is critical to know why it exists. This inquiry necessarily leads away from the nature of the poor as individuals to the nature of their social and physical environment. Poverty is not only a personal phenomenon, it is a social status. As such, while its effects can be measured on the level of the individual, its causes must be sought elsewhere. From the point of view of poverty alleviation the process of becoming is just as important as the state of being.

At the heart of poverty is the inadequate access of the poor to productive resources. Low incomes tends to reflect inadequate means of production, not incompetent producers. However, poverty in India is not simply a reflection of private resources. A broad range of "external" factors impinge on incomes, among them the following:

National Policies

One of the ironies of Indian development is that while no government wants poverty, many policies contribute to it—what is given in anti-poverty programmes is drained away by other policies. The poor do not always come out ahead in the balance—they are often net "donors" to the rest of society. Frequent reference is made to unsustainable forms of development—to urban over-expansion, industrialisation based on subsidies, and to public sector engorgement. What is less frequently realised is that the bill for these phenomena is often presented to the rural poor. Taxation of exports to sustain sectors with little export potential of their own and subsidised food imports to supply the urban population are policies that are often paid for by the rural poor. In many areas of India, exports are agricultural goods produced by small farmers. Here export taxes contribute to rural poverty. The same is true of "cheap" food imports, which depress the prices paid to small farmers for their food crops.

"Structural imbalance" is not only a recipe for increasing external indebtedness; it is also a recipe for increasing the poverty of the rural population. The political weakness of the poor in most areas is not only the basis for inadequate poverty alleviation programmes and policies—it is the basis for an actual transfer of their income to more socially influential groups. While it is often correctly asserted that the poor are the first to suffer from adjustments involving public social expenditure cuts, it is often the case that they also have the most to gain from the elimination of policy-based economic distortions that reflect social power rather than productive efficiency and potential.

Demographic Factors

Accelerated population growth is a long-term contributor to poverty. In India the incomes of the poor have declined, mortality rates are also falling, pushing the numbers up. In the meantime, land is becoming scarcer, plots more fragmented and the soil and pasture increasingly degraded. This phenomenon is not without its policy dimensions. As long as the poor remain undercapitalised, and essential determinant of household income is the amount of labour available to its household economic strategies favour large families. While population policy has a role to play, possibly more critical is a change in the economic environment. Access to capital and more secure income changes perceptions of the need for labour. In the medium—and long-term, population dynamics are driven by the underlying productive systems. As long as the production systems of the poor remain underdeveloped, population growth remains high, restricting even the future possibility of development.

Natural Resource Management and the Environment

If poverty is both cause and effect of rapid population expansion, so poverty is both cause and effect of many dimensions of degradation of the environment. Many of the rural poor, but by no means all, live in areas of extreme environmental fragility, a circumstance often prompted by high level of control by the better-off over more stable and productive resource areas. Here the poor are extraordinarily exposed to the dangers of erosion, whittling away at an already meager productive base. The threat is not entirely due to nature. Rather, poverty accelerates erosion. Without capital, the poor are frequently unable to invest in even traditional methods of soil and water conservation. And without sufficient land they are forced to shorten fallow periods, putting further strain on the resource base. As in the case of population growth, the result is strain not only on the poor, but on the entire Indian economy. Given the extremely limited economic alternatives, the solution to this problem is not to forbid the use of environmentally fragile resources to the poor; it is to change the conditions under which their use takes place. Access to conservation technology is important; but more so are security of land tenure and resources to invest.

Combating poverty means not only increasing the production of the poor, but also preserving and enhancing the long-term value of the resource they control. What this very often means, in practice is assisting the poor in reestablishing a stable relationship with fragile resource. Prevailing processes in many areas involve the gradual—and sometimes not so gradual—depletion of natural resources, to the detriment of all. Part of he answer to this is conservation. Part of the answer is also to provide viable economic alternatives to the poor, reducing their dependence on erosion-prone crop and livestock practices.

Exploitative Intermediates

The poor are not unaware of the pressure upon them, and also of means of overcoming them. Their ability to respond, however, is severely impaired by social powerlessness. The poor are surrounded by a dense network of public and private factors reducing their freedom of action, and actually draining what few resources they do have. Members of the network include traders and moneylenders capitalising upon the economic weakness of the poor, and engaging them in unequal exchanges. They also include public agencies either indifferent to the requirements of the socially uninfluential, or actively engaged in extracting "surplus" for use by other groups. Not to be excluded from this are organisations which are ostensibly "for" the poor, but which, in fact, serve as systems of containment and control.

25

Democracy and Poverty

Are they Interlinked?

Democracy assistance and poverty reduction are rightly becoming two focal—and related—issues for development assistance. Increasingly, many organisations, including intergovernmental, national and civil society, are focusing their work on these two areas. Futhermore, the relationship between these two issues is complex and ever changing. There is thus a need to develop methodologies of linking democracy assistance and poverty reduction at both the policy and programme levels. International IDEA (Institute for Democracy and Electoral Assistance) in cooperation with the World Bank and the United Nations Development Programme, is developing concrete strategies that address these two objectives in a mutually reinforcing way. Through an overall situation analysis followed by regional meetings in sub-Saharan Africa, South Asia, Latin America, the Caucasus and the Arab region, the Institute has marshalled evidence of some of the key problems that affect democracy consolidation and poverty reduction in these countries:

- Corruption and its undermining effect on popular confidence in public institutions;
- Continuing economic instability coupled with the lack of strategies for addressing the twin challenges of poverty and increasing popular participation in its alleviation;

- The extremely limited nature of citizen's influence on overall policy and decision-making processes despite the spread of formal democratic institutions;
- A trend in many post-communist states towards viewing growing poverty as a direct consequence of a transition to democracy.

In short, the evidence is not very encouraging for the prospects for democracy consolidation and poverty reduction. The critical step, International IDEA advocates is the development of an approach that not only seeks to put democracy assistance and poverty reduction on top of the development assistance agenda, but also to encourage all involved to treat them as twin elements of an integrated programme of action.

Through a focus on accountable governance, promotion and protection of citizenship and rights and increased popular participation, International IDEA believes that both democracy and poverty reduction can be addressed simultaneously. Policy recommendations are being developed and will be shared in the course of this year with governments, international organisations and civil society bodies.

International IDEA believes that democracy promotion can be used as a tool for fulfilling a variety of objectives. Democracy matters because it protects human right and preserves human dignity. But democracy also matters because it helps to address some of the most critical challenges facing states today: peace, development, economic growth and stability.

Democracy does not guarantee any one of these, but increasingly it seems to be a precondition for them in the long term. Thus, advocating democracy goes beyond being a moral issue; it becomes *fundamental* to advancing the well-being of people and the stability of states. International IDEA will continue to explore the link between democracy and the major issues facing society today—and continue to argue the case for democracy.

26

Richer or Poorer?

Achievements and Challenges of Ethical Trade

Ethical trade as an approach to supply chain management has mushroomed in recent years. Northern companies are becoming increasingly concerned with the 'ethics' of their operations and risks to reputation and productivity posed by bad employment practices in global supply chains. But can voluntary private sector codes really improve employment conditions in supply chains?

Ethical trade is one dimension of corporate social responsibility, bringing social issues into the mainstream of commercial supply chain management through the use of codes of conduct. It is sometimes confused with fair-trade which addresses terms of trading for smaller producers, and fosters greater responsibility in supply chain relations.

Ethical trade, on the other hand, focuses on workplace issues, requiring that supplier's in particular meet minimum employment, worker welfare and aspects of human rights standards.

Similar management systems are well established for product safety and environmental issues. Here we focus on the social dimensions of ethical trade and its codes of conduct yet the separation of social and environmental standards is increasingly artificial in global sourcing agreements. A plethora of codes are on offer. The most numerous are in-houses codes such as Nike's 233 company codes counted in 1999 and the figure is rising.

Suppliers have to comply with and pay for multitude of similar but different codes. Harmonising codes or establishing equivalence is on the agenda but has not yet halted the problem of 'code overload'.

At a broader level, industry-specific codes have also been developed. The US Apparel industry Partnership/Fair Labour Agreement adopted by a number of leading US merchandising companies is a good example. Industry standards are not new, as ISO and EMAS environmental management systems show. Building on ISO principles, Social Accountability International (formerly CEPAA) has developed SA8000. This is an independent social standard that can be used as an auditable code throughout the private sector.

Ethical trade is partly a response to consumer and campaigning group pressure in globalised economy. Alliances of companies, NGOs, trade. Developing codes of conduct through a multi stakeholder approach is a striking aspect of ethical trade, bringing together companies, NGOs, trade unions and some government departments. An example of this collaborative approach is the Ethical Trading Initiative (ETI) in the UK. The ETI's baseline code of conduct that corporate members from various industries must comply with as a minimum standard is more than just a code, ETI aims to provide a learning environment and sponsors pilot projects in developing countries to test different methods of monitoring and verification.

Codes of conduct need to be assessed in terms of content, implantation and impact. A number of professional auditing companies have moved into this area, some accredited to audit specific codes such as FLA or SA8000. Suppliers audited against a specific code undergo an inspection, and where non-compliance is found, have to take remedial action or risk failing the audit.

Social auditing is a complex process, however, and it can be difficult to spot work place abuse, such as sexual harassment or forced overtime. Workers have little confidence in a process that appears to be linked with management, and fear that reporting issues could risk their jobs. Advocates of the multi stakeholder approach argue that effective monitoring and verification of codes must involve local NGOs and trade unions in which workers have trust. Participatory social auditing also a means of raising awareness and of facilitating behavioural change, can help reveal serious management problems. But in many developing countries local organisations lack the capacity to participate: developing sustainable local systems of monitoring and verification remains an important challenge.

Do the advantages of multi-stakeholder approaches outweight immediate constraints? Ethical trade is a largely northern driven process, reflecting Western ethical thinking and priorities, Southern based initiatives, however, are expanding, raising the possibility of local ownership of codes, Collaboration poses challenges. Stronger relationships and better understanding are essential between southern and northern workers, producers, trade unions, and NGOs for codes to work globally.

But there is still scepticism as to the extent of the benefits that ethical trade might bring. Will increasing southern capacity to participate, as the ETI has done in its pilot project, help? Will building trust, confidence and dialogue achieve the objectives of ethical trade, north and south? Child labour is often more complex, however, than codes make it appear. Codes meet to address the conditions of all workers within the supply chain, including the least visible; partnerships must include all groups to address these limitations.

The role of government is hotly contested. Can a system whose credibility depends on under-resourced civil society actors, often excluding democratically elected representatives, maintain genuine credibility? If the boundaries between private sector and public sector roles are not defined, the list of private sector responsibilities will become unmanageable. Private sector initiatives are not a substitute for more comprehensive national or international development policies.

What are the consequences of codes? Do they encourage downsising or reinforce from large suppliers where compliance is more easily monitored? There is a risk that the gains of some will be at the expense of others.

Ethical trade has successfully begun forging partnerships to find solutions. While it might be wrong to assume that ethical trade can change the world, handled wisely it could make a world of difference for some. Yet it is not a panacea for development. Issues that remain unchallenged by ethical trade include:

- The exclusion of companies producing for domestic markets—often bigger employers.
- Underlying causes of poverty and social marginalisation.

27

Taking Poverty to Heart

Non-Communicable Diseases and the Poor

Non-Communicable Diseases (NCDs) are the leading cause of death worldwide. Their emergence as the predominant health problem in wealthy countries accompanied economic development. As a result, NCDs are often referred to as 'diseases of affluence'. But is this a misleading term? It suggests that these are not major problems for the world's poor, which is quite simply wrong, as this article illustrates. Is it time to rethink policy on NCDs?

NCDs include cardiovascular disease (CVD), such as stroke and heart attack, diabetes, chronic lung disease, cancer, diseases of bones and joints, and mental illness. The single biggest killer is coronary heart disease, followed by other CVDs, cancer and chronic lung disease. Diabetes is a major contributor to deaths form CVD, but also causes its own unique complications. Common risk factors for these conditions include smoking, physical activity, obesity and diets high in saturated fat and sodium and low in fruits and vegetables.

By 2020, NDCs will be the biggest cause of death in all regions apart from sub-Saharan Africa. It is predicted that in 2010, the number of people with diabetes worldwide will be double the level in 1995 and that the biggest increase (both proportionately and in absolute number) will be in poorer regions. CVD occurs at an earlier age in developing countries, increasing the potential adverse economic and social consequences.

NCDs are already major health problems for adults in the poorest countries of the world. Demographic data show that age-specific death rates from NCDs in Tanzania are higher than in wealthier countries. Mortality rates for some NCDs, such as stroke, are particularly high. However, while NCDs account for 80 per cent of adult deaths in developed regions, the figure is less than 30 per cent in Tanzania, reflecting the continuing burden of infectious disease. Countries like Tanzania suffer The worst of both worlds'. Even within a country, 'diseases of affluence' is a misleading term. A more accurate label is 'diseases of Urbanisation'. Several studies from developing countries show increased levels of high blood pressure and other NCD risk factors in urban compared to rural populations. Even within urban areas, the more affluent do not always suffer the greatest burden.

The rise of NCDs in developing countries is inextricably linked to economic and cultural globalisation. This is exemplified by the activities of multinational tobacco companies. Tobacco-related deaths will exceed the toll due to HIV and become the single largest preventable cause of death by 2020. Curbing the effects of globalisation on the prevention and treatment of NCDs will also require regulation of food and agriculture multinationals and the pharmaceutical and healthcare industries.

Much of the projected rise in NCDs is preventable, particularly that due to smoking, poor diet, physical inactivity and obesity. Early action in some populations could prevent the emergence of these risk factors altogether; in other, the challenge is to reduce established levels. Although it is unclear whether all major risk factors are equally important in every region, the strength and consistency of data on the core risk factors in several ethnic groups justify preventative action now.

Lessons from risk factor intervention studies in rich and middle income countries suggest that success requires.

- Broad intersectoral action
- Community participation
- Appropriate legislation
- Involvement of appropriate NGOs
- Health services changes—to manage those at high risk and promote public education.

Even apparently minor changes, such as a small fall in average population blood pressure, can have substantial benefits. However, some preventative pogrammes have produced disappointing results and almost all have failed to halt the ubiquitous increase in obesity. This highlights the difficulty of promoting healthy behaviour by individuals who are surrounded by barriers to change and inducements to lead an unhealthy lifestyle.

Health systems in developing countries face both a growing need for prevention programmes and increasing numbers of individuals requiring treatment. The complications of high blood pressure and diabetes can be reduced by the delivery of effective healthcare. Crucially, this entails:

- Partnership between patients and health professionals with the knowledge, ability and resources to take appropriate measures over many years.
- Cheap and effective drugs and the implementation of simple treatment protocols, as promoted by WHO and the CVD initiative of the Global Forum for Health Research.

An appropriate policy strategic framework is essential for such initiatives to be effective on a large scale. Even in the poorest countries people are already seeking healthcare for NCDs in both the public and private sectors, particularly in urban areas. Whatever the balance of priorities between different conditions, existing resources should be used as effectively as possible. Rapid evaluation methods can provide policy-makers with information on the current levels and quality of care and identify the main opportunities for improving health services.

The proper planning and co-ordination of NCD prevention and treatment, whether globally or nationally, requires up-to-date data on risk factor and disease levels—currently missing for much of the world. To address this lack, the WHO Non-Communicable Disease and Mental Health Surveillance section is promoting a standardised approach to enable comparisons across regions and over time, preparing the first ever 'world risk status' report for the major NCDs. This will provide a truly global perspective on the size and nature of the problem.

As this article has shown, NCDs are major health problems even in the world's poorest countries, including those regions where infectious diseases continue to take a huge toll. The NCD burden will grow substantially in low land middle-income countries over the next 10 to 20 years. NCDs will increasingly demand attention and require the right balance between competing priorities for prevention, cure and care. In meeting this challenge, national policy-makers will need to follow the lead of WHO and develop a strategic framework that plans for surveillance, prevention and appropriate health sector reforms.

28

Land Tenure

Securing Land for the Urban Poor

Around the world, especially in Asia and Africa, towns and cities are expanding rapidly. For the poorest people, finding affordable, safe and secure urban land for shelter has become increasingly difficult. This is because:

- Overall competition for land makes it increasingly costly;
- Central urban areas are being developed for commercial use;
- Natural features such as mountains or swamps limit physical urban expansion; and
- Meeting land management and planning standards (concerned with legality, technical and administrative accuracy) is expensive.

As a result, a large and increasing proportion of urban populations are forced to live in peripheral areas or occupy marginalised and dangerous locations. These settlements are often illegal and, providing inadequate shelter and lacking essential services only exacerbate the problems of the poor. Higher levels of ill health, unemployment and non-sustainable land-use often result. Furthermore, residents may also be under constant threat of eviction by government and exploitation by landowners.

Experience shows that, if residents in such areas feel secure and safe from eviction, they do over time improve their neighbourhoods. Recognition of, and granting of secure forms of tenure to previously illegal settlements often provides the incentive to communities to invest their resources in upgrading their housing and wider neighbourhoods. Security of tenure also brings the improved likelihood of basic infrastructure and other essential community services.

There is a wide range of urban land tenure systems. In many urban areas, including areas designated illegal by government, there are informal or customary tenure systems—these are often the commonest form of tenure and are expanding most rapidly.

While statutory or "legal" forms of tenure (for examples freehold or leasehold agreements) offer many advantages, such as full individual rights and security and access to formal credit systems, they can also cause the very problems they were intended to solve:

- Higher rental levels, which may displace existing renters;
- The selling out of the secure land to higher income groups;
- Encouragement of new illegal/informal settlements, as the poorest hope that they will also eventually get security of tenure;
- Encouragement of landowners and developers to hold land, without investing in its improvement or paying taxes on its increased value—which serves to attract even greater levels of investment and land price inflation.

In addition, if peoples' income remain low and the capacity of the banks or credit unions is weak, statutory forms of tenure alone may not necessarily stimulate neighbourhood improvements.

Consequently, careful analysis of existing systems of informal and customary tenure and property right is required, before embarking on major land management and tenure reforms. These can provide both acceptable levels of security and access to credit, which in turn stimulate improvements to local neighbourhoods. Before any decisions are made, tenure policies must recognise the likely impact on tenants, the poor and other vulnerable groups, especially women.

For these reasons, it is sometimes better to increase the rights of residents (e.g. by protecting them from the threat of forced evictions, or by increasing their access to essential utilities or credit), rather than assuming that they need freehold or leasehold titles.

Strategies for providing shelter now recognise the diverse nature of needs, and the positive contribution which decent housing makes to social and economic development at both national and local levels. They also recognise that the most effective way of mobilising the resources required is to encourage investment in housing by individuals, communities and the private sector.

Recent experience shows that many governments are now introducing positive approaches, which are market-sensitive and encourage more efficient use of available land. These include measures to encourage landowners and developers to allocate a specified proportion of units to low-income groups out of profits generated from planning permission granted by (and therefore partly created by) the government. Public-private partnerships and revisions to planning standards and administrative procedures have also demonstrated that it is possible to reduce the costs of access to land for the poor even under conditions of market-led development, thus reducing urban sprawl, the occurrence of slum settlements and levels of poverty.

29

City Politics

A Voice for the Poor

By 2020 the world's urban population will rise by almost 1.5 billion. Cities and towns house a growing proportion of poor people, partly because of the increased share of urban population of the total but also because economic recession and adjustment policies often hit poorer urban residents the hardest. Cities are associated with economic growth and wealth generation and yet inequality is high. Poor people generally live in substandard conditions, may not benefit from job creation, and suffer high levels of pollution, crime and violence.

How can city governments cope with the challenges of population growth and increased global economic competition, and meet the needs of poor residents/is urban governance responsive to the needs of the poor? Are the agencies responsible for city government, especially the municipalities, addressing poor people's needs? Are NGOs and people's organisations playing a greater role in service delivery? Or is their role one of advocacy and lobbying? If so, how do they relate to the formal political system? Can governments fulfil their responsibilities, including poverty reduction? How can the well-being of poor urban governance institutions priorities their needs? In assessing the responsiveness of city government to poor people, three key questions are addressed:

How Can the Poor Influence the Agenda of the Institutions of Urban Governance?

The influence of poor residents on decision-making is controlled, in part, by the formal political system. Democratisation gives people a vote. However, this vote means more when elected representative depend on the political support of poor people—where they are a majority, or are well organised, or where there is a ward-based system. If poor people are organised enough, to articulate their needs and demand a fair share of urban resources. NGOs can help poor groups organise better and provide support for networking.

Where poor people are not organised it does not mean they are politically powerless. Poor people in this situation, however, are prey to the disadvantages of patronage and unlikely to be included in formal consultative processes. For an electoral system to be truly responsive, specific mechanisms and channels, such as consultative and participatory processes at city an sub-city levels, are needed to complement representative democracy. Athough, these channels do not necessarily include the poorest or make a marked difference to resource allocation, pro-poor decisions are unlikely without them.

How Can Cities Finance Their Activities and Reduce Poverty?

Democratisation has not, in many countries brought allocation of financial resources or the revenue-raising capacity for local governments to fulfil their responsibilities. The responsiveness of city governments to poor people's needs thus depends, on whose voices are heard in the arenas of political decision-making. Responsiveness also depends on how available financial resources are allocated and how the programmes they finance are designed. There is scope, for city governments to increase property and business revenues, and to borrow for capital investment. Whether increased financial resources benefit poor people depends on how the demands of external investors and creditors are reconciled with the demands of poor residents; the willingness of politicians and officials to address the distributive implications of existing and planned spending; and efficient transparent financial management. If funds are made available to sub-city levels of government or if expenditure can be influenced by ward councilors, the funds might then be used to meet the priorities of poor residents.

What are the Necessities of Urban Living and How Can Access to Then be Ensured?

An Adequate Income: Work opportunities should be the top priority. City governments can, however, support the urban economy in general and the economic activities of the poor in particular. Firstly they can ensure that the basic services are efficiently provided. Secondly city governments can refrain from activities that destroy the assets and livelihoods of the poor, especially eviction of informal settlements and micro-enterprises. Savings and credit schemes can be more appropriately organised at a community level and supported by NGOs.

Land Ownership is a common aspiration for poor households. A home with secure tenure (not necessarily title) provides security, an appreciating asset, access to services, and a base for economic activities. Increasing the opportunities for poor households to gain access to a well-located plot of land is an important component of any poverty reduction strategy. Many never fulfil their dream and the needs of those who cannot, or do not wish to become home owners should not be neglected, however.

Local government is potentially more responsive to poor residents than are central government agencies, although this depends on the balance of political power and bureaucratic perceptions. The limited ability of the public sector to secure benefits for the poor from public-private partnerships in land development, suggest that more informal arrangements and the involvement of CSOs may be better ways forward.

Environmental Services: Land alone will not reduce poverty but must be linked to a healthy living environment—a package of appropriate and affordable environmental services, such as public transport, water and sanitation, solid waste collection, and energy for cooking and lighting. Rather than discussing appropriate standards, detailed issues of financing and affordability or how continued provision can be assured for each of these services, the research focused on how far decision making channels mechanisms and partnership arrangements ensure that providers are responsive to the needs and priorities of poor residents.

Collaborative planning and decision-making arrangements are one promising alternative, despite the current shortcomings of participatory budgeting. For responsiveness to the poor to be built in to such processes, local bureaucrats need to change their attitudes and working practices. Is it possible and acceptable for poor people to have to rely on their own resources their households and networks—resources that are very limited? Informal networks and links can, however, provide mutual support and access to politicians and bureaucrats, community associations thought not always present, inclusive or transparent, can play an important role in articulating poor residents views and in organising self-help activities. There is scope for formal representative community organisations, for informal links between peoples' organsiations and the power structures, and for networking between people's groups. NGOs can play an important role in developing the capacity of community organisations and in facilitating networking. Where NGOs play a role in service delivery. However, there is a danger that the resulting close relationship with local government detracts from their ability to empower poor people and challenge inappropriate policies. City governments, it is clear, cannot cope with the challenges of population and economic growth and respond to the needs of poor people alone. Only in alliance with other actors is there some hope that poverty can be overcome. For CSOs, many of which were forged during struggles for democratisation, this implies moving beyond confrontation to engagement. To form alliances between CSOs and city governments that put the interests of the poor first, poor people must be able to exercise their political rights.

30

Tapping the Market

Can Private Enterprise Supply Water to the Poor?

Over 170 million people have no access to clean water in urban areas throughout the world. Inefficient operation of state owned water companies is at the root of this injustice: gross over-staffing and political interference in tariff-setting have starved utilities of the resources needed to expand piped networks to impoverished areas.

The failure of the supply-driven approach has led to public private partnership (PPPs) designed to shift water utilities towards a demand-driven approach. Have these changes been accompanied by improved access to clean, affordable water for the urban poor? Has PPP improved equity in urban water supply? Are the new private sector operators addressing the needs of the urban poor in practice? This article examines the extent to which the urban poor have benefited or not from this newly emerging institutional arrangement.

The 'public' approach typically provides unclean water sporadically. It requires expensive, highly educated professionals, significant subsidies and tends to service clients on high and middle incomes whilst changing low tariffs. International financial institutions have failed to enable the public water suppliers to improve performance, either through massive investment in engineering, or through capacity building and institutional development.

At the other extreme is an efficient, demand driven, customer-oriented approach, the 'small scale independent providers', delivering water to cities' inhabitants, with near 100 per cent bill collection efficiency. Promoting local employment and servicing the poor, this approach has, until recently, been ignored by water sector professionals. Lacking regulatory oversight, however, their prices are typically 10 to 20 times higher than those paid by high-income consumers connected to the network. Which of these providers are most effective at serving the poor? The starting point is to recognise the evidence suggesting that the urban poor are prepared to pay to meet their survival and convenience needs for water.

Notwithstanding the rhetoric to the contrary by some trade unions and NGOs, initial results from larger cities indicate that the efficiency of 'privatised' water utilities has improved markedly: leakages are down and net revenue is up through improved billing and collection and reduction in personnel. Whether this is due to the alleged benefits of private sector investment or the freedom of foreign operators to manage without being beholden to employee and entrenched political interests is not yet clear.

Has the Extension of the Network to Poor Communities Been Speeded Up?

Concession contracts require private operators to meet coverage targets. But the decisions on the direction of network expansion to meet targets are usually left to the operators as regulatory bodies are usually formed after contract signing. So are poor communities given priority? Technical criteria based on cost-effectiveness in the construction of main pipes, commercial criteria based on pressure from property developers, and political criteria based on vote-winning tactics may all conflict with social criteria based on the pressing needs of poor communities.

Is the Cost of Household Connection Affordable by the Poor?

Even where operators do give priority to extending the piped network into poor communities, difficult issues arise over the financing of secondary pipelines, household connections and meter installation. Techniques are evolving to reduce the cost of connection so as to ensure affordability for all. These may take the form of tripartite arrangements whereby the public sector provides grants for the purchase of materials, community groups provide voluntary labour, and the private operator provides technical assistance. NGOs may contribute by providing crucial skills in team management and local understanding not usually found in the bureaucratic culture of public sector institutions or the techno-professional culture of private water companies.

Is the Water Tariff Affordable by the Poor?

Even where poor communities have been connected, there is no assurance that householders can afford the water charges. Many have no job security or regular income. Billing arrangements need to be shortened from the monthly norm to fit the short-term financial horizon imposed by household poverty.

Property-based tariff structures still discriminate against the poor by providing far cheaper water per litre for high-income households consuming large volumes for swimming pools and sprinkler systems. Reforms should positively discriminate in favour of the poor, with some cross-subsidisation from richer to poorer households. However, where the initial life-line block is greater than average monthly domestic water use by the poor (perhaps over $6m^3$ per household a month), middle income groups benefits the most. A single volumetric tariff for domestic consumers with subsidies aimed at facilitating water connections rather than consumption is now being recommended.

This article focuses on the three major challenges for the sector in the new millennium:

- First it is crucial to develop regulatory skills to oversee this affordable expansion. The key capacity constraints facing municipalities—usually the public sector partners in PPPs;

- Second is the need to incorporate the skills of small-scale independent providers;
- Thirdly it is important to move beyond the metropolitan capitals, to where cross-subsidies are more achievable, and address the water needs of the urban poor in the myriad of secondary towns in the south.

31

Consuming the Future

Now that we are to reach six billion of us, it is a good point to check again on what sort of lifestyles we pursue and what is the environmental impact of those lifestyles. It is curious that we have spent several decades being concerned about the growing numbers of humankind while not giving at least an equal amount of attention to the levels of living we aspire to, and how many natural resources we chew up thereby and how much pollution and waste we cause.

Everybody is a consumer of sorts. True, every fifth person scarcely qualifies for that designation, consuming goods worth less than $1 per day. Conversely, every seventh person qualifies for a designation of super-consumer, with a cash income at least fifty times greater. These latter are the people who, through their carbon dioxide emissions, are disrupting everybody's climate dozens of times more than the average citizen of One Earth. Fair Play, anyone?

Much as the have-nots seek to match the have's, it is plain their efforts will not work out for a long time to come, at best. If every Chinese person were to consume just one additional chicken per year and if the said chicken were to be raised primarily on grain, this would account for as much grain per year as all the grain exports of the number two exporter, Canada. If the Chinese were to raise their per-capita consumption of beef, now only 4 kgs per year, to that of Americans, 45 kg, and if the additional beef were produced largely in feedlots after the manner of the United States, it would account for as much extra grain as the entire US grain harvest, less than one-third of which is exported. Because of its recent climbing up the food chain toward a meat-based diet, China has become one of the world's leading importers of grain. The global grain market today is around 200 million tons per year, and shows scant scope for significant increase.

As a further measure of its ambitions, the Chinese government has designated the auto industry as one of five industry "pillars". Today China has fewer cars than Los Angeles. If per-capita car ownership, together with oil consumption, were to match that of the United States, China would need 80 million barrels of oil per day—by contrast with the world's 1996 oil output of 64 million barrels of oil per day. The surge in carbon dioxide emissions would be unprecedented.

All this notwithstanding, there are already some 250 million newly affluent people in China. They are people with a household income equivalent to perhaps US$20,000, and enough discretionary income to enjoy the perquisites of the good life as perceived by these nouveaux riches. Top of the shopping lists are meat and more meat, followed by cars whether big or small. These are the badges of success: they show you have arrived.

The new consumers in China are matched by at least 200 million in India, and tens of millions in South Korea, Taiwan, Malaysia and Thailand (the recent economic setbacks have not permanently punctured the economic bubbles). Then there are 200 million more in Brazil, Argentina, Venezuela and Mexico, and more again in Hungary and other countries of Eastern Europe, also Turkey. Put them all together and they total about as many as the 800 million long established consumers in the ultra rich countries (the OECD grouping). When the current economic hiccups in Asia are left behind, the ranks of the new consumers can be expected to rise rapidly.

But they cannot hope to become super consumers. Where would all the extra gain come from? How could the global climate tolerate the huge additional pulse of carbon dioxide? There are all kinds of other environmental reasons to suppose that environmental constraints will become all the more constraining. True, technology could help moderate the environmental impact. We could enjoy twice as much material prosperity while using only half as much natural resources and causing half as much pollution and waste. But the new consumers will want to pursue the American dream to the hilt, and it is hard to see that the best technologies could enable huge numbers of affluent aspirants, perhaps two billion people by 2010, enjoying even half the material prosperity of Americans with average household incomes of $40,000.

But is it true "prosperity"—mental and emotional as well as material? Or is the American dream becoming a nightmare with its harried lifestyles and declining leisure time, where the shopping mall is the ultimate Mecca, and the good life is a case of piling up goodies?

In any case, we cannot expect the new consumers to forego their "rightful share" of affluence unless the long-time affluent agree to cut back on their environmental ruinous lifestyles. It is these communities that must offer a strong example, and soonest. Where is the political leader who will espouse the new vision, however much it may be perceived as the ultimate vote loser?

32

Myths and Illusions

The tide of precarity is rising steadily, so that people who have never been poor no longer regard poverty as a distant prospect but as one so close that it could engulf them at any moment.

In 1989, the fall of the Berlin Wall was rightly welcomed because it marked the collapse of a system that provided a degree of equality but rejected freedom. Today there is a strong possibility that the system gradually spreading all over the world—a kind of neo-liberal fundamentalism—may also collapse. In its obsession with freedom, vital though freedom is, this fundamentalism disregards equality, a term which should not be regarded here in purely static and statistical terms, but as something dynamic and ethical. Equality can only be truly practised in a context of social solidarity or to borrow from the vocabulary of the French Revolution of fraternity.

On the one hand, we have a world that is immensely rich in resources, possibilities, knowledge and experience; its constituent societies are freer and more dynamic than ever. There is an extraordinary potential for everyone to live a better life. But at the same time, new and ever higher walls are being built both between peoples and between social groups within individual countries. We are experiencing a travesty of development, which is creating a world bipolarised into extremes of wealth and poverty.

The most common reactions to this disastrous situation are very often the result of two misapprehensions. The first can only be described as ideological or doctrinaire since it is not based on the facts as they can be observed. It says that since the dominant system of values and things is by definition more than satisfactory, the persistence of impoverishment is merely a temporary blip. Enough time has elapsed, however, for us to see that this is not the case, including in countries where this system has been part of the established order for more than a century. One statistic is particularly eloquent. In just over 30 years, world production has approximately doubled, but the gap has more than doubled between the income of the 30 per cent of world's people living in the richest countries and the income of the world's poorest 20 per cent, according to the United Nations Development Programmes.

The second misapprehension stems from another form of blindness and illusion, namely the belief that poverty can be regarded exclusively as a moral issue, as if it had no other kind of implications for those who are not poor. Globalisation is, however, a two-way process. It enable the countries of the North to export their values and their paradigms as well as their goods and capital to the countries of the South, but it also makes them much more vulnerable to the backlash of crises that afflict these countries. Even in the North, the cult of competitiveness is undermining situations once considered extremely stable. The tide of precarity is rising steadily, so that people who have never been poor no longer regard poverty as a distant prospect but as one so close that it could engulf them at any moment.

Because of inadequate socio-economic development, the extraordinary upsurge of democracy over the past 30 years remains a very fragile process, and there is a risk that the trend may be reversed. When hunger, disease and ignorance prevail, citizens' participation in decision-making becomes either non-existent or a mere charade. Democratic institutions become empty shells, representational bodies existing in form only and devoid of real significance

Social divisions caused by economic distortions exacerbate the failures of democracy which in turn pose serious threats to civil order within countries and to peace between nations. It is high time to face these obvious facts.

33

Population Growth and Jobs

Since mid-century, the world's labour force has more than doubled-from 1.2 billion people to 2.7 billion, outstripping the growth in job creation. As a result, the United Nations International Labour Organisation estimates that nearly 1 billion people, approximately 30 per cent of the global work force, are unemployed or underemployed (working but not earning enough to meet basic needs). Over the next half-century, the world will need to create more than 1.9 billion jobs—all of them in the developing world—just to maintain current levels of employment.

As economists often note, while population growth may boost labour demand (through economic activity and demand for goods), it will most definitely boost labour supply. During the next 50 years, almost 40 million people will enter the global labour force—defined as those between the ages of 15 and 65 seeking work-each year. Between 1995 and 2050, some 1.9 billion additional jobs will need to be created to absorb these new would-be workers. The most pressing needs will be found in the world's poorest nations—a sobering example of the vicious cycle linking poverty and population growth.

As the children of today represent the workers of tomorrow, the interaction between population growth and jobs is most acute in nations with young populations. Nations such as Peru, Mexico, Indonesia, and Zambia with more than half their population below the age of 25 will feel the burden of this labour flood. In the Middle East and Africa, 40 per cent of the population is under the age of 15. Since new entrants into the labour force were born at least 15 years ago, measures to reduce population growth have a delayed effect on the growth of the labour force, highlighting the urgency of taking action on population.

Nowhere is the employment challenge greater than in Africa, where at least 40 per cent of the population lives in absolute poverty. Although 8 million people entered the sub-Saharan work force in 1997, by 2030 this resource-scarce region will have to absorb more than 17 million new entrants each year. Over the next half-century, Nigeria's labour force is projected to grow by 246 per cent and Ethiopia's will soar by 337 per cent—both faster than growth of the general population. At current growth rates, the size of the labour force in sub-Saharan Africa will more than triple by 2050.

As a result of unprecedented population growth and increasing acceptance of female participation in the work force, the number of people seeking jobs in the Middle East and North Africa, a region already plagued by double-digit unemployment rates, will double in the next 50 years. In Algeria, where unemployment stands at 22 per cent, the labour force is growing at a staggering 4.2 per cent annually, and the number seeking work will more than double by 2050. Egypt alone will need to create 26 million more jobs by 2050 as its total population hits 115 million.

Nations throughout Asia will also see phenomenal increases in the numbers seeking work, including Pakistan, where the work force will grow from 70 million in 1998 to 205 million by 2050. Over the next 25 years, India will add nearly 10 million to its work force each year. During the same period, China will add nearly 6 million annually due to population growth alone, compounding the work shortages caused by the current flood of migrants to China's coastal cities and by massive layoffs—estimated at more than 30 million—as state-run operations are scaled back.

Nations are hard-pressed to educate and train rapidly growing numbers of young people in marketable skills for the global workplace. Moreover, meeting the basic needs of a growing population draws scarce foreign exchange and other resources from investments in education and job creation. Throughout the world, young people entering the work force are increasingly faced with unemployment and social marginalisation. In most societies, unemployment rates for those under 25 are substantially higher than for older people.

Surplus farmland once served as a traditional source of employment for growing populations, as new land could be ploughed to generate work and income. However, global percapita Greenland has dropped by half and considerably more in certain nations since 1950. Moreover, the machanisation of agriculture fuels the exodus of job seekers into the world's urban areas, where unemployment is often most acute heavily reliant on natural capital in the past, future job creation will require massive amounts of financial capital to jump-start the industrial and service sectors.

As the balance between the demand and supply of labour is tipped by population growth, wages—the price of labour-tend to decrease. And in a situation of labour surplus, the quality of jobs may not improve as fast for workers will settle for longer hours, fewer benefits and less control over work activities.

Employment is the key to obtaining food, housing, health services, and education, in addition to providing self-respect and self-fulfilment. Rising numbers of unemployed people could drive global poverty and hunger to precarious levels, fueling political instability.

Bibliography

Books

A.C. Pigou (1960). *The Economics of Welfare,* Macmillan & Co. Ltd., London.

Ahluwalia, Montek, S. (1985). "Rural Poverty, Agricultural Production and Prices: A Re-Examination" in John Mellor and Desai Gunvant, M. (eds.) *Agricultural Changes and Rural Poverty,* The John Hopkins University Press, London.

Amartya Sen (1995). *The Hindu,* 6th November, Interviewed by Ramamanohar Reddy, Chennai.

Betellei, A. (2000). *Chronicles of Over Time,* Penguine Books, New Delhi.

Carr, Maryn *et al.,* (1997). *Speaking Out; Women's Economic Empowerment in South Asia,* Vikas Publications, New Delhi.

Chakravarty, Sukhamoy (1989), *Development Planning, The Indian Experience,* Oxford University Press, New Delhi.

Charsely, S.R. and G.K. Karanth (1998). *Challenging Untouchability. Dalit Initiative and Experience from Karnataka,* Sage Publications, New Delhi.

Chinnadurai, K. (1986). *Evaluation Study of Implementation of IRDP,* State Bank of India, Coimbatore.

Dantwala, M.L. (1996). *Dilemmas of Growth: The Indian Experience,* Sagar Publications, New Delhi.

Delige, R. (1999). *The Untouchables of India,* Berg, New York.

Desai, B.M. and N.V. Namboodiri (1993). *Rural Financial Institutions: Promotion and Performance,* Oxford and IBH Publishing Company Pvt. Ltd., New Delhi.

Dev, S. Mahendra (1999), "State Interventions and Women's Employment", in T.S. Papola and Alakh N. Sharma (Eds.). *Gender and Employment in India;* Vikas Publishing House Pvt. Ltd., New Delhi, pp. 373-411.

Dharm Narain & Sen, A.K. *et al.* (1989), *Studies on Indian Agriculture,* Oxford University Press, New Delhi.

Frencine Fournier (1997), *Foreword, Poverty and Participation in Civil Society.* Edited by Yogesh Atal of Else Oyen, Abhinav Publications, New Delhi.

George Psacharopoulos and Moureen Woodhall (1986). *Education for Development: An Analysis of Investment Choices,* Oxford, New York.

Griffin (1979). *The Political Economy of Agrarian Change,* The Macmillan Press Ltd., London.

Griffin Keith (1978), *International Inequality and National Poverty.* The Macmillan Press Ltd., London.

Griffin Keith (1981). *Land Concentration and Rural Poverty,* The Macmillan Press Ltd., Hong Kong.

Gunnar Myrdal (1968). *Asian Drama—An Inquiry into Poverty of Nations,* Pantheon, New York.

Gunnar Myrdal (1970). *The Challenge of World Poverty: A World Anti-Poverty Programme in Outline,* Pantheon, New York.

Gupta, D. (2000). *Interrogating Caste: Understanding Hierarchy and Difference in Indian Society,* Penguine Books, New Delhi.

Haq, Mahabub Ul (1978). *The Poverty Curtain: Choices for the Third World,* Oxford University Press, Bombay.

Haq, Mahabub Ul (1997). *Human Development in South Asia,* Oxford University Press, New York.

Harper, M. (1998). *"Profit for the Poor",* Oxford and IBH Publishing Co., Delhi.

Hirway Indira (1984). *Programmes for Poverty Eradication: A Critique of Target Group Approach,* Sardar Patel Institute for Economic and Social Research (Mimeo).

Holcombe, Susan (1995). *Managing to Empower: The Grameena Bank's Experience of Poverty Alleviation,* Oxford University Press, Dhaka.

IFMR (1984). *An Economic Assessment of Poverty Eradication and Rural Unemployment Alleviation Programme and their Prospects,* Madras.

Jackson Dudley (1972). *Poverty, MacMillan Studies in Economics,* MacMillan, London.

Karmakar, K.G. (1999). *Rural Credit and Self-Help Groups, Micro-Finance Needs and Concepts in India.* Sage Publications, New Delhi.

Kaushik Dasu (1984). *The Development Economy: A Critique of Contemporary Theory.* Oxford University Press, Delhi.

Khan Azizur Rahman & Eddy Lee (1984). *Poverty in Rural Asia,* Asian Employment Programme (ARTEP), Inernational Labour Organisation, Bangkok, Thailand.

Kuznets S. (1965). *Economic Growth and Structure,* Heinemann, London.

Lewis, A. (1966). *Development Planning,* Allen & Unwin, London.

Mahammad Haan Khan (1981). *Underdevelopment and Agrarian Structure in Pakistan,* A West View Replica Edition, West View Press, U.S.A.

Maheswari, S.R. (1985), *Rural Development in India,* Sage Publications, Delhi.

Minhas, R.S. (1974). *Planning and the Poor,* S. Chand & Company Limited, New Delhi.

Mukta Mittal (1995). *Women Power in India,* Anmol Publications Pvt. Ltd., New Delhi.

Myrdal Gunner (1968). *Asian Drama, Volume III,* Twentieth Century Fund, New York.

NABARD (1999). *Banking with the Poor: Financing Self-Help Groups,* CGM, NABARD, Hyderabad.

NABARD (1999-2000), *NABARD and Micro-Finance,* Mumbai.

Nanda, Y.C. (2000). *Role of Banks in Rural Development in the New Millennium,* National Bank for Agriculture and Rural Development, Mumbai.

NCERT (2000). *Human Development in South India,* Oxford, New Delhi.

Parthasarathy, G. (1982). "Integrated Rural Development Concepts, Theoretical Base and Contradiction, in *"Development Planning and Policy"*, Edited by Gupta D.B., *et al.,* Wiley Eastern, New Delhi.

Rahman, Hossain Zillus (1998). *Poverty Issues in Bangladesh,* Power and Participation Research Centre, Mimeo.

Rai & Tandon (1999). *Voluntary Development Organisation and Socio-Economic Development,* Indian Economic Association, 82nd Conference Volume, Amritsar.

Sakuntala Narasimhan (1999). *Empowering Women, An Alternative for Strategy from Rural India,* Sage Publications, New Delhi.

Sen A.K. (1984). Poverty and Famines: *An Essay on Entitlement and Deprivation,* Oxford University Press, Delhi.

Shylendra, H.S. (1999), *Promoting Women's Self-Help Groups: Lessons from an Action Research Project of IRMA,* Anand, India, Working Paper No. 121.

The World Bank (2000-2001). *World Development Report,* Oxford, New York.

Todaro Michael, P. (1977). *Economics for a Developing World,* Longmans, London.

Todaro Michael, P. (1990). *Economics for a Developing World,* Second Edition, Longmans, New York.

Von Braun, J., Bayes, F. and Akhter, R. (1999). *Village Pay Phones and Poverty Reduction.* ZEF Discussion Papers on Development Policy No. 18, Centre for Development Research, University of Berlin.

Von Pischke, J.D. *et al.,* (1983). *Rural Financial Markets in Developing Countries: Their Use and Abuse,* John Hopkins University, Baltimore, U.S.A.

Yogesh Atal (1996). *Poverty and Participation of Civil Society,* Abhinav Publications, New Delhi.

Zeller, Manfred and Manohar Sharma (1998). *Rural Finance and Poverty Alleviation,* Food Policy Report, International Food Policy Research Institute, Washington DC, USA.

Journals

Amitava Mukherjee (1999). *Out of the Abysis. The Challenge Confronting Some Civil Society Actors,* Indian Economic Association, 82 Conference, Amritsar.

Awasthi, P.K., *et al.,* (1986). 'IRDP: Receptivity and Reaction', *Indian Journal of Agricultural Economics,* Vol. 41, No. 4, October-December.

Bagchee, Sandeep (1987). 'Poverty Alleviation Programmes in Seventh Plan: An Appraisal', *Economic and Political Weekly,* Vol. XXII, No. 4, January 24.

Bardhan, P.K. (1973). 'On the Incidence of Poverty in Rural India of the Sixties, *Economic and Political Weekly,* February.

Bhat, Mazi, P.N., *et al.,* (1999). Finding of National Family Health Survey Regional Analysis, *Economic and Political Weekly.* Vol. XXXIV, Nos. 42 and 43. Oct. 16-22/23-29.

Chambers, Robert (1994). *"Poverty and Livelihoods Whose Reality Counts?" Overview Paper II, UNDP Stockholm Roundtable,* "Change: Social Conflict or Harmony?" 22-24 July.

Copertake, James G. (1996). *The Resilience of IRDP: Reform and Perpetuation of an Indian Myth, Development Policy Review,* 14.

Dantwala, M.L. (1983). "Rural Development: Investment Without Organisation', *Economic and Political Weekly.*

Desai, A.R. (1987). 'Rural Development and Human Rights in Independent India, *Economic and Political Weekly,* Vol. XXII, No. 31.

Desai, B.M. and J.W. Mellor (1993). "Institutional Finance for Agricultural Development: An Analytical Survey of Critical Issues", *Food Policy Review I, International Food Policy Research Institute, Washington, DC, USA.*

Ghosh, D.K. (1995), Group Cohesiveness in DWCRA Groups: An Application of Sociometric Approach, *Kurukshetra*, May-June.

Govil, R.K. (1982). 'Micro-Level Planning and Rural Development', *Kurukshetra.*

Grewal, R.S. et al., (1985). 'Impact of Integrated Rural Development Programme on Rural Women in Bhiwani District of Haryana', *Indian Journal of Agricultural Economics,* Vol. XL, No. 3, July-September.

Hara Gopal, G. & Balaramulu, Ch. 'Poverty Alleviation Programmes: IRDP in an Andhra Pradesh District, *Economic and Political Weekly,* Vol. XXIV, Nos. 35 & 36, September 2-9.

Hirway Indira (1984). *Programmes for Poverty Eradication: A Critique of Target Group Approach,* Sardar Patel Institute for Economic and Social Research (Mimeo).

Jain, S.C. (1986). 'Poverty Alleviation Programmes in India: Some Issues of Micro Policy', *Indian Journal of Agricultural Economics,* Vol. XLI, No. 3, Conference Number, July-September.

Karmakar, K.G. (1999). *Rural Credit and Self-Help Groups: Micro-Finance Needs and Concepts in India,* Sage Publications, New Delhi.

Kumar Rajinder, *et al.,* (1986). 'Impact of Credit on Income, Employment and Capital Formulation of Rural Poor', *Indian Journal of Agricultural Economics,* Vol. 41, No. 4, October-December.

M.S. Kallur (2001). 'Empowerment of Women Through NGOs: A Case Study of MYRADA Self-Help Groups', Indian Journal of Agricultural Economics, Vol. 56, No. 3.

Mosley, P. and R.P. Dahal (1985). "Lending to the Poorest: Early Lessons from the Small Farmers: Development Programme, Nepal", Development Policy Review, Vol. 3, No. 2.

NIRD (1985), 'Employment and Income Generation Through IRDP, NREP and DRM', *Journal of Rural Development,* Vol. 4, No. 5, March-September.

Owusu, K. Opoku and William Tetteh (1982). "An Experiment in Agricultural Credit: The Small Farmer Group Lending Programme in Ghana", *Savings and Development,* Vol. I, No. 1.

Rajaram Das Gupta (2001). "Working and Impact of Rural Self-Help Groups and other forms of Micro Financing", *Indian Journal of Agricultural Economics,* Vol. 56, No. 3.

Rajasekhar, D., (1996), "Problems and Prospects of Group Lending in NGO Credit Programme in India", Savings and Development, Vol. 20, No. 1.

Sinha, S.P. & Prasad Jagadish (1980). 'Special Programmes for Weaker Sections: An Evaluation', *Indian Journal of Agricultural Economics,* Vol. XXXV, No. 4.

Stiglitz, J.E. (1990), "Paper Monitoring and Credit Markets", *The World Bank Economic Review,* Vol. 4, No. 3.

Thakur, D.S. (1977). 'Rural Development in India: Past Experience and Tasks Ahead', *Indian Journal of Agricultural Economics,* Vol. XXXII, No. 3, July-September.

The Hindu, 11th May 2002, Chennai.

Yaron, J. (1992). *Successful Rural Finance Institutions,* World Bank Discussion Paper, 150, Washington, DC, USA.

Reports

Amitava Mukherjee (1999), *Out of the Abysis. The Challenge Confronting Some Civil Society Actors,* Indian Economic Association, 82 Conference, Amritsar.

APDPIP (2000), *On Andhra Pradesh District Poverty Initiatives Project Appraisal Document (PAD), Report No. 20089,* South Asia Regional Office.

Chief Planning Officer (2001). *Hand Book of Statistics, Mahabubnagar District,* Mahabubnagar.

Chief Planning Officer Collectorate (2000). *Hand Book of Statistics, Krishna District,* Machilipatnam.

Chief Planning Officer Collectorate (2001). *Hand Book of Statics, Chittoor District,* Chittoor.

CIRDAP (1998). *Increased Household Income and Rural Women in Asia, Impact on Status and Activities*, Dhaka, Bangladesh.

CIRDAP (1998). *Poverty Gender and Participation*, Dhaka.

CIRDAP (1999), *Rural Development Report, Centre on Integrated Rural Development for Asia and Pacific*, Dhaka.

CIRDAP (2000). *Poverty Gender and Participation*, Dhaka.

CMIE (2000). *Profile of Districts, Economic Intelligence Service*, October, Mumbai.

Government of Andhra Pradesh (1998). *Annual Report of the Commission of the Rural Development*, Hyderabad.

Government of Andhra Pradesh (1999). *Annual Report of the Commission of the Rural Development*, Hyderabad.

Government of Andhra Pradesh (1999). *New Series on State Domestic Product*, A.P., Hyderabad.

Government of Andhra Pradesh (2001). *Provisional Population Totals, Series 29*, Hyderabad.

Government of Andhra Pradesh (2001) *Statistical Abstract*, Hyderabad.

Government of Andhra Pradesh (2001). *Strategy Paper*, Hyderabad.

Government of India (1991). *Census of India*, New Delhi.

Government of India (1997-2002). *IX Five Year Plan*, New Delhi.

Government of India (2001). *Provisional Population Totals*, New Delhi.

Government of India (1974). *Towards Equality—Committee on the Status of Women in India.*

Government of India (1998, 99). *Reports of the Commissioner of SC and STs*, New Delhi.

Haq, Mahbub Ul. (1997). *Human Development in South Asia,* Oxford University Press, New York.

Holcombe, Susan (1995). *Managing to Empower. The Grameen Banks' Experience of Poverty Alleviation,* Oxford University Press, Dhaka.

IFAD (1996). *The State of World Poverty, Rome for a Discussion on the Process and Structural Causes of Poverty,* see Rovert Chambers (1983). Rural Development, Putting the Last First, London, Longmans, One of the Best Discussions on how these Perpetuate Poverty.

IFAD (2001). *Rural Poverty Report, The Challenge of Ending Rural Poverty,* Oxford, New York.

Indian Bank (2002-2003). *Annual Credit Plan, Krishna District (A.P.),* Vijayawada.

International Fund for Agricultural Development (IFAD) (1992). *The State World Rural Poverty—An Inquiry Into its Causes and Consequences,* New York University Press, New York.

ISACPA (1992). *Independent South Asia Commission or Poverty Alleviation.*

NABARD (1999). *Annual Report, Mumbai.*

NABARD (2000): *Annual Report,* Mumbai.

NABARD (2001): *Annual Report,* Mumbai.

NIRD (1994). *Rural Development Report: Rural Employment,* Hyderabad, Andhra Pradesh.

NIRD (2001). *National Conference on SHG Movement in the Country & Swarnajayanti Gram Swarozgar Yojana (SGSY).* National Institute of Rural Development, Hyderabad.

PEO (1985). *Evaluation Report on Integrated Rural Development Programme,* New Delhi.

RBI (1984). *Implementation of Integrated Rural Development Programme*—A Field Study.

SAARC (1992). *The Independent Source Asian Commissions of the SAARC on Poverty Alleviation,* Dhaka.

South Asian Association for Regional Co-operation (SAARC) (1992). *Meeting the Challenge, Report of the Independent South Asian Commission on Poverty.*

The World Bank (1990). *World Development Report,* Oxford, New York.

The World Bank (1991). *Gender and Poverty in India,* Washington DC.

The World Bank (1999-2000). *World Development Report 1999-2000,* Oxford University Press, New Delhi.

UNDP (1994). *Human Development Report,* Oxford, New York.

UNDP (1996). *Human Development Report,* Oxford, New York.

UNDP (1997). *Human Development Report,* Oxford, New York.

UNDP (2000). *Human Development Report,* Oxford, New York.

World Bank (1990). *World Development Report—Poverty,* Oxford University Press.

Yerramaraju, B. and Firdausi, A.A. (1995). *Evaluation of DWCRA in Prakasam District.* Sponsored by Government of Andhra Pradesh. Administrative Staff College of India, Hyderabad.

Others

Government of Andhra Pradesh, *Vision-2020,* Hyderabad.

Government of India (1985). *Five Year Plan Documents (The Seventh and Eighth Five Year Plans 1985-95),* New Delhi, The Planning Commission.

NABARD (1984). *Study of Implementation of IRDP (Mimeo),* Bombay.

Government of Andhra Pradesh (1999). *Vision-2020*, Hyderabad, India.

Government of Andhra Pradesh, *Guidelines for Swarnajayanti Gram Swarozgar Yojana, Panchayati Raj and Rural Development Department*, Hyderabad.

IXth Five Year Plan (1997-2000).

The Hindu (2002). April 27, Chennai.

The Hindu, Vision 2020.

INDEX

N

O

P

U

V

W

Z